Ted Maltese - *Cover Art*
Mary Beth Berg - *Book Design & Illustration*

Wayne Adams

Downhill Is Where the Fun Is

Downhill Is Where the Fun Is
Why Your Upper Years Should Be the Best Years

Wayne Adams

Part One

Getting Older Doesn't Mean Getting Worse

Contents

Part Two

Why the World Needs Seniors

Part Three

Ways to Help Make the Journey Fun

Preface

Okay, I'll admit that I may be on the downhill slope. I know this because I get so many birthday cards that joke about my being "over the hill." Surely, that many people wouldn't tell me something they didn't mean, would they? Not at the high price of greeting cards these days.

What I don't understand, though, is the negative image many people have of this stage in life. It seems that "over the hill" has come to mean "nothing good happens anymore." Why? Hasn't downhill always been more fun than uphill?

When you were a kid, did you get a kick out of trudging laboriously up the hill towing your sled through the snow, or was it more fun to skim down that hill like a small bolt of lightning? When you rode a roller coaster, did you scream with delight while you slowly chugged upwards, or did that happen after you topped the crest and began hurtling down?

It turns out that life works a lot like those sleds and roller coasters did. You get a job, pull your sled to the hill, or select a seat on the roller coaster. Then starts the long, seemingly endless grind as you climb. It's not terribly exciting, although the view does expand somewhat as you go higher. Then you notice that your progress is slowing down, just about stopping. You're frustrated. Nothing is happening, and nobody seems to care.

Suddenly, you retire from that job, reach the top of the hill, or top the crest of the roller coaster. You break free of the gravity, cogs and gears that have controlled your progress until now. You throw your arms in the air and embrace the wind as you speed along. Whether you're sledding, riding the roller coaster, or traveling through life, this is not the time to complain that you're going downhill. My friend, downhill is where the fun is!

Of course, how much fun you have on this trip depends partly on how you travel and partly on who you travel with.

Much of what I know about downhill travel I learned in the third grade. My dad worked that winter in the small town of Cannon Falls, Minnesota. It never seemed to stop snowing that year. The city even closed off one very hilly street to auto traffic and reserved it for us kids to slide on. Every day after school, I loped over to that hill pulling my sled. It was like having an amusement park in our own neighborhood.

I soon learned there were boundaries to be observed even in this seemingly carefree environment. The right-hand edge of the street was claimed by a lone skier who fussed if we interfered with the neat grooves he carefully etched into the snow with his skis. The left side of the street belonged to a raucous group of high school kids who whooped it up on a huge homemade bobsled, with its front runners guided by an old steering wheel salvaged from a car. The rest of us spent our afternoons belly-flopping on sleds down the center.

I was lucky. The old hand-me-down sled I inherited from a cousin steered better and ran faster than most of my friends' sleds. Its qualities almost got me into big trouble, though. We were always supposed to stop our downhill runs before we got to the business district. One day my sled was going so fast that I continued under the barrier, across Main Street, and then down another hill for a few more blocks. It was sheer luck that I wasn't run over. (It probably helped that gas was rationed in those World War II days, which cut down the amount of traffic to just about zero.) Despite being a foolhardy third-grader, I did stop and think after that stunt that even when racing downhill, you occasionally need to use some common sense.

After we moved back to Minneapolis, I continued my sliding career at the nearest golf course. Skiers were still the aloof elite, maintaining their own runs separate from us sledders. There were no bobsleds, but their place was taken by toboggans for those boys and girls who preferred to slide as a group. Toboggans were almost impossible to steer, but the frequent need to bail out in a writhing pile of bodies to avoid crashing into a tree seemed to be a big part of the fun for those teenagers. I didn't fully understand that part until later.

These days, as Hallmark and my friends frequently point out, I'm going downhill figuratively instead of literally. However, the same general principles I learned in the third grade still seem to apply.

Some of us prefer to take our downhill trip alone, following well established trails. You could even say ruts. Some of us like to journey in a group. Paradoxically, this can make for more thrills and spills while at the same time giving a feeling of greater security. Some of us are in between, taking our own individual belly-flops but informally sharing the experience with our companions. And we all need to try to strike some balance between enough common sense to stay healthy and enough risk-taking to have fun.

People my age just need to keep things in perspective. Sure, we're going downhill. That's not necessarily a bad thing. As we look at those who are still climbing up, we may envy their looks or health or careers. But let's not envy them their place on the hill.

They still must focus on the struggle of their climb. They can only see the part of the hill right in front of them. And they seem to feel the need to take themselves pretty seriously.

We've been there, done that. Now we're past that stage. Being over the hill means we can see more. We should even be able to stand back a little bit and look at life with the amusement it surely deserves.

The essays in this book take a light-hearted look at life from the viewpoint of those who have managed to overcome the immaturity of youth and maybe even the frustrations of middle age.

Some parts may sound like complaints about the way the world (or nature) treats us. But hey, complaining is a big part of the fun in life for some of us. If you're my age, you'll understand that. If you're a youngster, get used to it — someday you'll be just like us.

Whatever the subject, each piece is designed with one goal in mind: to remind you that downhill should be fun. Climb aboard, and let's enjoy the ride.

—Wayne Adams

Part One:

Getting Older Doesn't Mean Getting Worse

Don't begin overly fretting
if the things you do seem to get harder,
it might be your body is getting
not decrepit, but just a bit smarter

The Best of Times, the Worst of Times, the Best of Times Again

Most people have the idea that happiness in life follows the usual bell-shaped curve. After all, we seem pretty unhappy when we're very young (crying at bedtime and all that). Then there's the storm and stress period of teenage angst. We ought to be happiest in our 40s, after we've settled into marriage and career and are poised to make our fortune. In later years comes the inevitable descent into decrepitude, which seems too depressing to think about.

Actually, it works in pretty much the opposite way. Instead of a bell-shaped curve, happiness follows a U-shaped curve. The happiest times are at the early and late ages and the unhappiest years are in the middle. American men are least happy at age 49, American women at 45. Strangely enough, it's not just codgers like me who make that claim. It's a scientific fact.

Years ago, David Blanchflower from Dartmouth College and Andrew Oswald from the University of Warwick in the UK published a paper on the subject. They analyzed statistics from the U.S. General Social Survey from 1974 to 2004 and the Eurobarometer surveys from 1975 to 1998. These surveys included an incredible total of 500,000 people from the U.S., France, Belgium, Netherlands, West Germany, Italy, Luxembourg, Ireland, Great Britain, Greece, Spain, and Portugal. With that many people reporting, there couldn't have been much doubt: The further you are from middle age, the happier you are.

Why do people above middle age get happier as time goes on? The researchers suggested that one possibility is the likelihood that we eventually learn to adapt to our strengths and weaknesses, and thereby come to terms with the goals we're not going to accomplish in life. Another possibility they mentioned is that happy people just tend to live longer, and so those of us who are still around to answer questionnaires in our 60s and beyond were just overly cheerful to begin with. A third reason they thought of is that at this stage we've already seen so much tragedy in our lives that we put greater value on what few blessings we have left.

Do any of those explanations sound like a reason to be deliriously happy? I certainly don't think so either. In that case, what's the real answer? I think we have to look at both the high and low ends of that U-shaped curve in order to really understand what makes people happiest at those extremes.

My feeling is that folks at retirement age are sort of comparable to those in their mid to late teens. Both groups are embarking on a new and exciting stage in life. They're looking forward to having more freedom than before. They're able to travel more freely, either because they've just gotten their first driver's license or because their AARP discount saves money on cruises. Those in their seventies are even happier, as are the kids around age ten or so. Nobody expects you to do much, so life is pretty carefree. You've got a lot of free time to indulge in whatever games and hobbies you like. And the people around you are the same people you've loved for as long as you can remember.

For those in their eighties and above, life is like the incredibly happy times of a preschooler. When you get up in the morning, life is a blank slate, to do with as you wish. Play games, romp in the garden, watch cartoons, or sit and do nothing. Anything is permitted. And everybody talks to you in a voice full of exaggerated cheerfulness. What's not to be happy about? I can only imagine the unlimited happiness and contentment that must be experienced by centenarians and toddlers. So if you're at the stage mistakenly called the prime of life, all I can say is that my sympathies are with you. If you're in your first or second childhood, congratulations!

Changes as We Age May Mean Our Bodies Are Wising Up

When I was younger, I never worried about how I would cope with the physical changes that come with growing old. Well, of course the main reason was that I never imagined getting old would happen to me. But as it turns out, I needn't have worried anyway.

The reason is that, as your body ages, the changes that happen to it are just an accentuation of things you're already used to. Your body acts pretty much like it always did, only more so. For example, when you're a teenager the sight of a pretty girl can set your heart racing. When you're my age, it only takes a little spell of atrial fibrillation to accomplish exactly the same thing. No other person is required.

When you're young, something scary can make your hair stand up. When you're older, even if nothing scary happens your hair may not only stand up but it could walk away and not come back. I don't quite understand why it acts like that. During their summer vacation, kids find that a lot of time in the sun tends to make their hair lighter in color and their skin darker. When you're old, your body doesn't need the sun to accomplish this. Hair turns white and skin develops what we call liver spots indoors or out, summer or winter. Apparently the body gets more efficient at these processes as time goes on.

As you grow from baby to adult in size, your skin has to somehow keep stretching to fit your ever-enlarging body. It must be a struggle for it to keep up. Maybe that's what led to those growing pains you had as a child. After you reach seniorhood, though, your skin manages not only to keep up with your current size, but to plan ahead. It tends to grow enough so that it can remain comfortable even if you continue to become larger. It does this by creating folds (sometimes called "wrinkles") that provide built-in room to expand. Isn't that clever? There are a bunch of other imaginative new adaptations our bodies sometimes come up with to help us cope better with modern life.

Young people, as you know, are constantly exposed to painfully loud music. Older bodies learn to defend against this problem by developing ears that are much less sensitive to sound. It's a little harder to understand why our eyes choose to become blurrier as we grow older. My theory is that this makes the folks we associate with look more attractive to us, which improves our romantic lives. And what could be a more important adaptation than that?

An Ability that Always Improves with Age

Although I usually can't remember where I left my glasses a half hour ago, for some strange reason I can remember an awful lot of things that happened when I was just a toddler. One special memory I have is my first trip to the circus.

I don't recall being tremendously impressed by the animals or clowns, but I'll never forget the aerialists. They did a stunt that blew my mind. It wasn't any of the gyrations and acrobatics they performed on the trapeze or tightrope. Their most amazing trick came before that stuff even began. As I sat there at floor level and watched them make the long climb up to the top, I saw them slowly shrink in size. They were tall adults when they started out, and were teeny little dolls when they got way up high! How did they do that? Obviously, I had no understanding of perspective at that stage in life. My eyes, which didn't need glasses in those days, showed me very clearly what was happening. My mind just didn't quite know how to process their apparent shrinkage in size as they moved further away. It took a while to develop an understanding of perspective. I like to think that this process continues all through life, and that as we age our sense of perspective keeps improving all along.

As children, we soon learn that people only LOOK smaller when they move a few yards further away from us. This knowledge not only enables us to understand a circus performance, but it becomes helpful when aiming a water pistol or playing tag.

As teens, we realize that, although our parents are no longer bigger than us, for some reason their authority remains large. Even a mom who has to crane her neck to glare into your eyes can still put you on time out.

As young adults, we learn that people can loom large even when you can't see them at all. You may be completely separated from a special someone, but she can fill your senses and thoughts to overflowing. As middle-agers busy with our careers, we come to understand another paradox of perspective. Some co-workers who sit next to you are really not as close to you as they seem. When it comes time to compete for a promotion, you'll see how distant they really are. And as we acquire the wisdom of seniorhood, we comprehend that nobody in the world is more than a few degrees of separation away from us and that we're all the same size in God's eyes. So far, that seems about as complete an understanding of perspective as I've managed to attain.

Isn't it nice to know that, even as parts of us grow weaker with age, there are still some things, such as our sense of perspective, which continue to improve as we move up through the years? I'll make a note of that comforting idea, if I can just remember where I put my glasses.

Kids Get the Young Bodies but Youthful Minds Are Ours

It's time to share a little secret about aging. There's quite a bit of evidence that the only real youthfulness these days is found among people my age and older.

Old folks used to say it was too bad that youth was wasted on people too young to appreciate it. That may not be entirely true anymore. Oh sure, youthful bodies are still doled out to the same age group as before. But these days, youthful attitudes often appear to be distributed to a much older crowd.

Kids no longer get much of a chance to be young. Grade school children carry the weight of the world on their shoulders – literally. Doctors report an epidemic of juvenile back problems because kids' backpacks are so loaded down with books, assignments, computers, and grooming aids. Now there are formal guidelines on how much weight can be piled on these tender shoulders. And after kids totter home under the weight of their responsibilities, what do they do? They attend play-dates arranged by adults. They participate in sports governed by Little Leagues with uniforms, coaches, and referees. Their little day-planners are crammed with meetings, practices, and tournaments. Oh, I can see how it all came to be this way. The backpacks are heavy because parents and teachers want to provide kids with all the skills and tools they'll need to succeed in their demanding future careers. As for that over-organized spare time, caring adults have set up all those programs so their kids can have fun and develop their muscles while staying safe in these chaotic and dangerous days.

It's just too bad that today's youngsters are missing the spontaneity and freedom that my generation had when we were their age. My bunch had it lucky. Our spines were not bent by heavy packs. At the most, we toted home a couple of books and notebooks. There were no calculators, computers or heavy metal lunch boxes to lug.

Certainly, none of us felt the need to carry a lot of stuff around to beautify our hair or prevent zits.

After school, sports were played in streets or vacant lots with teams chosen on the spur of the moment. We would have died if an adult had come along to boss us around as coach or umpire. That would have turned sports from play into some kind of after-school chore. Disputes over balls and strikes, penalties or fowls were negotiated (at the top of our lungs) by the entire group. We invented instant replays. Although we lacked video, we developed the ability to mime disputed plays after the fact, over and over again if necessary. Having grown up under these conditions, my generation probably lacks the respect for organization that one needs to adjust to life in a modern bureaucracy. We're more inclined to experiment on our own, to try new things just for the fun of it, to question the rules. Doesn't that sound like a description of youth?

Our childhood tradition of loud but harmless conflict probably makes us a bit more likely to be naughty about minor regulations. But I'm inclined to think that it also makes us much less likely to snap and commit major violence. That sounds like youth too.

"Old age is not for sissies," my dad often pointed out when he was in his 90s. He was right when it comes to physical and social matters. But if you judge by enthusiasm, imagination, and the ability to create their own fun, a lot of people in their "second childhood" have a better deal going for them than those who are still struggling through their first.

Seniors Can Cope Better in Today's Crazy World

I'm afraid I have bad news for men below retirement age. Brace yourselves, kids. The more the world changes, the more it becomes evident that only seniors are well adapted to live in it. (This may not apply to women, since they're outside my field of expertise. Anyway, they seem able to adjust to everything. Or maybe everything finds it necessary to adjust to them.)

Let's look at an example of how older guys are better adapted than young ones to the world of today. Take transportation. Young men have an awful lot more trouble than we do in flying anywhere. To begin with, they have more problems getting through security. When it comes time to take their shoes off, most young guys have to sit down to unlace them and then later to tie them again. Duffers have long since converted to slip-ons, or at the very least shoes with Velcro closures.

Next, young guys must take the laptops out of their backpacks or briefcases to send them through the scanner in a separate plastic bin. We seniors just bring along an old novel or back copy of the Saturday Evening Post we've been meaning to read some day. No need to unpack them. Young guys are more likely to have big belt buckles as well as pockets full of coins, money clips, and cell phones that trigger the security alarm. By the time they make it through the checkpoint after several tries, they must rush to the end of the conveyor belt in hopes that nobody has run off with their laptop. Seniors have very little cash, forgot to bring their cell phone, and have switched from belts to suspenders. We just stroll right through.

Once on the plane, young people tend to fidget and feel the need to walk up and down the aisle during a long flight. We seniors have mastered the art of remaining motionless in a reclining seat for hours without it causing us anxiety. Young people are also more likely to have problems after their plane arrives at its destination. I heard somewhere that lost luggage is up something like 25% over what it was a few years ago. A senior is better able to cope with lost luggage, because we're already used to slouching around wearing the same outfit every day for a week. This senior advantage in travel doesn't just apply to flight. Let's look at driving. The biggest change that drivers need to adjust to these days is the astronomical cost of gas. The young guys roaring down the freeway in their SUVs pay a fortune just to get to work. We older folks drive our small sedans at the speed where their gas mileage is highest – 30 to 40 miles per hour. We therefore make a lot fewer stops at the pump. You'd think the drivers swooshing past us making those rude finger gestures would catch on to our wisdom.

I'm sure there have been many periods in human history when the world was ideally suited for the young, the athletic, the excitable. This just doesn't happen to be one of them. All I can say to my youthful friends and relatives is gee, I'm sorry about that. But maybe you should consider patterning your behavior on the codger culture. You're eventually going to do it anyway.

Father Time, Not Cupid, Should Symbolize Love

When Valentine's Day approaches, greeting-card sellers turn happily to thoughts of love. For the rest of us, love tends to be on our minds pretty much all year long.

Yes, love is even in the thoughts of us older folks. In fact, I would say ESPECIALLY us, which will come as a big surprise to the younger generations. Although love is usually portrayed as a winged infant brandishing a bow, the fact is that the older you get, the more you know about love. It would be more accurate to picture love as looking like a white-bearded Father Time, walking hand in hand with Mother Time. Oh sure, when kids are hit by their first crush it's such a momentous discovery that they think they've invented something never before experienced by mortals. Given the powerful emotions aroused, this is understandable – but inaccurate. It's happened before. Even their own parents and grandparents had first crushes, shocking as that may seem.

Later, when young adults begin a sexual relationship, the explosion of passion and intimacy is another fantastic new discovery. Nobody older could possibly be experiencing anything like that! Well sure, at one time their parents must have had sex, but certainly not since conceiving their children. After that, Mom and Dad undoubtedly settled into platonic domesticity, their sexual mission in life accomplished. Sorry, kids. Even though it makes you exclaim *"Eeeeuuuw!!,"* your parents and even your grandparents might still make love. It works pretty much the same as when they were your age, except that now it may be the gal instead of the guy who asks "Did you remember to take your pill?"

Sex gets best of all after you and your spouse retire from your jobs. Think about it. You can make love any time of the day or night. The only intruders who might scamper down the hall and into your room are your dog or cat, and they won't be particularly shocked by what you are doing. But that's just one part of the landscape of love. As the years go by, couples learn additional ways to express their feelings. Without giving up the emotional attachment that came with that first crush or the passion that exploded from their first sexual union, older couples continually move together into new territory. They find the understanding that enables them to finish each other's sentences. They discover how, without exchanging a word, to know when their partner wants to leave the party and go home. They learn the acceptance that helps them overlook each other's wrinkles and silly habits. So even if they get to an age where their bodies seldom or never can perform the physical act of making love, their minds, hearts, and souls are probably better at love than ever.

When a relationship begins, it may be true that "Love is blind." But if love really lasts, it lets you clearly see and accept each other – imperfections and all. I'm thinking of when my folks were in their nineties and living with us. They began each day with my mother lying on the couch, her feet in my father's lap, as he read the newspaper to her (beginning with the obituaries, of course, given their age). She had macular degeneration, and couldn't see well enough to read the paper herself. He had very poor short-term memory, and tended to read a column several times, often repeating the same comment on an obituary like, *"Oh my, she's very young looking."* My mother would just smile, wink at me, and let him repeat it over and over.

That's a side of love that a couple can't achieve until they've been together for many years. I'm glad that I got to see my parents display this tender care for each other. I think it was a special blessing given to them to compensate for the fact that they had never engaged in the physical aspect of love-making since the spring of 1934, when I was conceived. Never mind what I said earlier about older people and sex. These are my PARENTS I'm talking about, for heaven's sake! *Eeeeuuuw!!*

Join the Party!

I no longer remember many things that my college professors told me, but one has always stood out. In a psychology class, our teacher said that when people get senile, it's kind of like they get a little drunk. Both conditions tend to exaggerate your basic personality traits. The professor explained that if you're naturally a bit gruff, you're likely to get very cranky when you drink – or later, when you get senile. If you're a pleasant, happy-go-lucky kind of person, you turn into a life-of-the-party drunk or a very cheerful old-timer. The idea seemed very intriguing, and I started looking around me for evidence. At the time, I didn't know many old people, although I knew several classmates who drank a bit too much. The professor's theory seemed to work out. Alcohol did seem to exaggerate natural personality traits in some of the people I partied with.

These days, I don't know many who drink a great deal, but I do know quite a few people who are getting older. Not senile, you understand, but older. And the professor's theory still seems to work. You don't have to actually become senile to have your basic personality start coming out more strongly. Just getting a bit older seems to do the trick.

Our friends who were sort of enthusiastic in high school now seem to lead extremely lively, adventurous lives today. Those who were rather quiet and laid back in high school now spend much of their day dozing in their recliner.

I think there's really good news in all this. Think of it this way: If growing old is like attending a party, by the time you get to be my age every night is practically New Year's Eve! How you choose to react to a party is up to you. Pick a fight, put a lampshade on your head, or conk out in the corner. But how can you not like being at a party? Therefore, aging has got to be fun! Nevertheless, I can't help but wonder how my personality will be affected as I get REALLY old. I guess a good clue would be to look at how I react to imbibing some alcohol. I don't ever pick fights or put on crazy bonnets. I'm more likely just to get talkative and then sleepy.

Well, I'd like to expand on all this, but I guess I've talked long enough already. Besides, I feel the need for a nap. Funny, I haven't had anything to drink today. You don't suppose I'm getting...

Aging Is Just a Matter of Quality Control

At long last, I ran across some information about aging that might actually be helpful. Usually, scientists' pronouncements don't suggest anything you could actually do about aging besides brood. They'll say something like, *"Cells are programmed to die after they divide so many times."* What good does it do to know that? But I read somewhere that folks at Scripps Research Institute in San Diego explained things in a way I can sort of understand. They said that after middle age, it's not that our cells stop dividing but that they replace themselves with imperfect copies. The result is sagging skin, graying hair, and aching backs. Aging, said these researchers, is really a disease of quality control.

Now, anybody who has worked for a living has probably had to deal with quality control issues. It's something we ought to be able to handle. The trouble is, different kinds of businesses take very different approaches to quality control. We'll have to decide which ones to use. I think I'll try them all.

One of my sons used to be in charge of quality control for a software company. What little I understood of his job is that he was supposed to keep the product from going out the door before it was ready. This sure seems like a principle I could apply.

I belong to several committees and organizations that insist on having meetings at 7:30 in the morning. Now I can tell them that my quality control team won't allow me to go out until my body is ready, which will be at least 10:00. This should lead to stress-free, well-rested, happy little cells that can pay more attention to what they're doing. How can the poor things be expected to divide properly with all the distractions of fighting rush hour traffic and then listening to overly cheerful speakers at that ungodly hour?

I used to have a neighbor who worked in quality control for a manufacturing plant. His job apparently involved using a micrometer to compare what was coming off the assembly line with perfect examples of what the part should ideally look like. This approach might be useful too. I understand there are magazines and even movies that show fine examples of youthful skin cells. I'll just explain to my wife that these are necessary for my quality control studies. I don't believe it's necessary that the samples I study be the same gender as me. Skin is skin, right?

The corporation I used to work for took a third approach to quality control. They simply came up with a new slogan every year telling how much we loved our customers and extolling what a great job we did for them. I guess this is called making "positive affirmations." I think I'll try this too, although I hope nobody hears me telling myself in the mirror how young I look.

Even if these methods fail, the idea of taking a businesslike approach to aging seems a positive thing. For example, I used to think I went bald some years back. Now I realize that, in order to compete successfully in today's fast-paced global economy I simply had to restructure my head by laying off a few thousand redundant follicles.

Remembering the Important Stuff

Those of us who are blessed with excessive maturity tend to be way too nice to the rest of the population. For example, when they make fun of us for not remembering something, we just passively accept the criticism. We even worry that the young punks are right; there must be something wrong with us. Nonsense! Let's try a simple test. Ask one of those young people how many presidents they personally remember. What did they look like, what did their voices sound like? Maybe they can recall all the way back to Ronald Reagan or Jimmy Carter. Well, I remember them all the way back to FDR. Even if you only go back as far as Eisenhower or Kennedy, you've got a lot more presidents to remember than these young kids. So it's not that our memories don't work anymore; it's just that they're busy remembering a lot more stuff.

We carry around more world, local, and family history. We've been more places, seen more things, and learned more hard lessons. We've loved more and been angry more. We've had to build a lot of rooms, closets, and attics in our heads to hold it all. Our memories aren't feeble; they're hauling an immense load.

If you see a guy carrying a hod of bricks, would you criticize him for not stooping to pick up a penny off the ground? No! He's already lifting more than enough. (If you're a young twerp you probably don't even know what a "hod" is, so just take my word for this.)

Then why criticize me if I don't add your phone number to my already overloaded memory bank? I'm sure your number is every bit as nice to have as that shiny penny on the ground, but I'm not willing to risk spilling the incredible load I'm already carrying in order to add it to my collection. There are calendars and PDAs to help me recall minor things like doctor appointments (at least, when I remember to look at the day's schedule). People I converse with are usually cooperative in reminding me who the heck they are. This frees me to devote my built-in memory to the heavy stuff. Things like FDR's jaunty cigarette holder, Fibber McGee's overloaded closet, and Humphrey Bogart's menacing monotone. No PDA is big enough to hold REAL memories. So from now on, don't feel embarrassed when you forget someone's name, or what day it is, or your PIN number. Instead, applaud yourself for the vast amount of more important stuff that you DO remember.

What Am I, Chopped Liver? Sadly, No

You hear an awful lot these days about the "sandwich generation." They're the people who find themselves trying to take care of not only their kids but also their parents or grandparents. One of the reasons you hear about this so much now is that parents and grandparents are living longer. Thus they're more likely to get to the stage where they need some help. The other reason you hear about it so much is that Baby Boomers are currently the ones who are likely to find themselves in the middle of the sandwich. Because of their sheer numbers, whatever has happened to the Baby Boomers at any stage of their lives has blossomed into a really big deal. When they started school, the educational system we'd always had was suddenly considered inadequate. The nation started a frenzy of school construction, followed by all sorts of experiments in new teaching methods. Young people had always experienced their hormones acting up at a certain age, but the Boomers felt they had discovered something altogether new, and dubbed it the "Sexual Revolution." All through history, adults have worked for a living and pursued material success. But the Boomers plunged into it like another new discovery, and developed the competitive "Me Generation." Possessions became highly important. If it didn't seem like you could afford some expensive toy, why you just needed to apply another new slogan: "Think outside the box." Outside-the-box thinking means that there are really no limits — not as long as you have credit cards.

Middle-aged people have always felt a little frustrated, but when the Boomers hit that stage it was amplified with a new name: "Mid-Life Crisis." And so now the Boomers find themselves, bless their hearts, worrying about family members both younger and older than themselves. Thus we have their newest term, the "Sandwich Generation." Well, like all the other Boomers' discoveries, people have lived through this one before too. We just lacked their wonderful ability to come up with a catchy name for it.

My wife Mickey and I spent quite a few years in the middle of that sandwich. Her mother, who suffered from emphysema, lived with us the last two years of her life. We still had some of our kids at home, so it was definitely a sandwich situation. It wasn't entirely easy to get used to that new layer of responsibility. For example, Mickey would take her mother to the shopping mall in a wheelchair. Out of force of habit, when she wanted to pause and look at something, Mickey would keep rocking the wheelchair forward and back. That technique had always worked very well for keeping a toddler in a stroller from getting too impatient. Her mother recognized the maneuver and laughingly pointed out, *"You don't really need to do that for ME, you know."*

A few years later, my own mother and dad lived with us for over a decade. Our six kids were out on their own by then, but you never really get to stop worrying about them so we were still in the middle of the sandwich.

Now, we're the family's oldest generation. I still like to think of myself as that essential ingredient in the middle of the sandwich. Maybe a lean hunk of beef. Or I've sometimes been described as sort of a hot dog. Heck, I'd even settle for being a savory mound of chopped liver. But instead, it seems like I've somehow turned into that slice of bread on top. I'm not sure just when that happened. I first noticed it several years ago when we had a big snowstorm and our daughter called. She forbade me to go out and run the snow blower myself. She and our son-in-law came over that night to take care of our driveway.

Okay, I was a little dismayed at this apparent demotion. Still, I have to admit that being the slice of bread on top does have some comforts. The word "loaf" is beginning to take on a whole new meaning. It no longer implies a lack of ambition. For a slice of bread like me, it speaks about my purpose, my role in life. Thanks, kids. Let's see, should I aspire to be whole wheat, rye, or pumpernickel?

Can You Pass the "Old" Test?

I ran across an article that explains how to decide when an older person has reached such a state of decline that the family needs to intervene. I thought I'd better read it, because I'm sure my kids studied it closely. There was good news and bad news. According to the article, the warning signs that you're no longer coping include:

1. A shortage of food in your refrigerator.

No problem here. Actually, our family sometimes intervenes because we have the opposite situation. My wife is a fantastic cook. She also tends to make meals big enough to serve our six kids and eleven grandkids just in case they happen to drop in for dinner. Our refrigerator overflows with leftovers too wonderful to throw out. There are also likely to be several doggy bags dragged home from restaurants (which all seem to insist on serving oversized meals nowadays). When our youngest son visits, he makes pointed inquiries as to how long something has been in there before he'll risk trying it. Every so often, our youngest daughter volunteers to come over and clean it out for us. All in all, I'd say that by the "refrigerator" measure we are the direct opposite of old.

2. A rapid change in eating habits or weight.
Again, I think we're okay by this measure. True, there's been a change in eating habits. My wife no longer makes desserts or keeps any ice cream in the house (unless, of course, some grandchildren are coming over). However, this doesn't seem to have resulted in a noticeable change in weight. In fact, I used to find my inability to lose weight discouraging. That was before I learned that it helps lower our score on the senility scale.

3. Mismatched or soiled clothing.
Okay, this is one where I score alarmingly high. But there are extenuating circumstances. My clothes have never matched, since I'm color blind (which has nothing to do with age). They tend to get soiled because drops of soup or gravy that might ordinarily land on a napkin in my lap now splat onto my slanting shirt front instead. This follows from my success in maintaining my weight (Item 2 above, which you will recall scored as a positive thing).

4. Poor housekeeping,
such as stacks of unopened mail or stains on the carpet. We get mixed results on this one. Being a very busy person, I do tend to ignore any mail that doesn't look like a check. My wife is quite good about throwing away ads and junk mail, especially if they have to do with anything electronic that might be tempting to me. We're both pretty bad, however, when it comes to magazines. She has a policy against throwing away any publication containing a recipe. For my part, I'm an avid student of current events and popular culture. Therefore, I

like to completely finish reading a news magazine before starting on the next week's issue. I've gotten a little behind. At this point, I'm still reading about Clinton's election campaign. (Bill Clinton, not Hillary.) Occasionally, either my stack of news magazines or my wife's stack of cooking magazines topples over and knocks a coffee cup onto the carpet. So we do score fairly high on piles of mail and carpet stains. However, this is really caused by her interest in gourmet cooking and my efforts to reach a deep understanding of modern history. I don't think age has much to do with it, do you?

5. Poor short term memory.
No age-related problem here. For some reason, I've never been able to remember names, so there was nothing whatsoever to diminish in that regard. As for what my wife refers to as my "woolgathering," that's not really a memory lapse. It's a sign of my ability to focus intensely on the really important stuff I'm thinking about and put aside minor issues such as where I left my glasses or what street I was supposed to turn on to get home.

Generally, I don't think we score too badly on the age-decline test. Of course, in my case it's mostly due to the fact that I've been sloppy and forgetful from childhood on. Either I've managed to preserve my youthful outlook, or I was born precociously old.

Am I Becoming My Crotchety Computer?

Despite all the problems it's been giving me, I think I'm getting fonder of my old computer. As such machines go, it's pretty long in the tooth. I've owned computers since I bought my Commodore SX-64 in the mid 1980's. It was followed by a long line of successors that took their turns sitting on my desk, kitchen counter, and lap. My experience indicates that, in the lifetime of computers, one computer year equals about fifteen human years. That would make my current five-year-old laptop equivalent in age to a 75-year-old person. It definitely is showing its age. Maybe that's why I kind of identify with it.

One symptom it has developed: occasional episodes of fuzziness. Every so often, the image on the screen goes all blurry and grainy and filled with lines. When I move the mouse, the arrow on the screen leaves a powdery trail. The problem doesn't seem to be with the screen, but just that every so often the computer has trouble concentrating. Well, I can hardly be too hard on the fella. I sometimes have trouble keeping things in focus too. A tendency to woolgather is to be expected at a certain age. When the computer has one of these episodes, the solution is to reboot. Sometimes it works the first time, and sometimes I have to try it several times before it wakes up in a clear mood. I can understand that too. It sometimes takes me a few false starts before I completely wake up in the morning.

As you might expect of a computer feeling its age, mine has slowed down. It plods through programs that it used to race through. It even needs a minute or so to get around to printing out a page, whereas my wife's computer (a young adult in human years) begins kicking out a page instantly on the same printer.

I'm the last person who should be faulting anyone or anything for moving too slowly. Over the years, I've taken to heart the wisdom in the story of the tortoise and the hare. I used to stride down the street like the wind, eyes set straight ahead on some distant goal. Now, I take my time when I walk. I'm geared more for examining and enjoying each leaf and pebble along the path. (Or at least I would be if I didn't wear bifocals.)

The most annoying symptom of my computer's age is that it

doesn't always stay up running and performing when I want it to. I could be in the middle of something important or enjoyable to me, and it just goes down at the most inopportune time. Let's see, where was I going with this part? Oh, never mind. Anyway, you might be wondering why I don't just replace the old relic with a new computer. Well, it has some features and abilities I use that a new one would lack. At the time I'm writing this, I still use several programs designed for older versions of Windows, but which probably wouldn't work with the latest operating system. If I buy a new computer, I may have to buy and learn a bunch of new programs.

In somewhat the same way, we older people come with a few capabilities that aren't readily found in the rosy-cheeked younger generation. Like my old programs, we actually know how to get things done using the systems that have always made the world go around in the past. Older folks can contribute experience, perspective, and, yes, maybe even some wisdom. It would be a shame if employers, organizations, and spouses decided to replace all members of my generation with glossy newcomers. I guess that's why I kind of identify with my crotchety old computer, and intend to keep it around as long as possible.

You're Not Aging as Much as Society Is

Does it bother you that sometimes you just don't seem to be able to do a lot of things that you used to? Maybe even the addition of technical aids like canes and golf carts don't entirely compensate for the changes that happen over the years. Well, don't feel bad. These things can be depressing, but it's important to put them in perspective. This isn't just happening to you, but to all of society. A lot of everyday things that used to be routinely expected now seem to be too difficult. For example, I heard the Postal Service is floating the idea of discontinuing mail delivery on Saturdays to cut expenses. It seems like deja vu all over again. Does anybody else remember the time when they had to cut down from two deliveries a day to one? Looking back, it seems incredible what kind of service we used to receive. For the price of a 3¢ stamp, we got two mail deliveries a day. And there weren't automated machines to read and sort the addresses. Somehow, humans did it all. Postage is now many times the cost of what it was then. Why can't there be comparable service? It's apparently a lost art from the past, like building pyramids.

Shopping is another area where our ancestors received better service. Women in my mother's generation took the bus or streetcar downtown to do their shopping. Public transportation ran every few minutes, and cost about 15¢. Stores employed a lot of people to help you pick things out. When you made a purchase, you never carried the parcel home. The day after your shopping trip, the store delivered everything you bought, without charge. When delivery costs started to become bothersome, stores ran a campaign to push the revolutionary idea of carrying home some of the stuff yourself. "The parcel you carry gets home first," was the slogan. Eventually, of course, department stores abandoned their free delivery service altogether.

When I was a youngster, it was routine to phone in your grocery order and have the store deliver it within an hour or two. Dairy products and bakery goods showed up at your door every morning, usually delivered in a wagon drawn by a horse that greatly enjoyed the flowers that we kids fed it (without our mothers' knowledge, of course). Dry cleaners picked up and delivered as part of their service. There are very few companies attempting to provide these services today. The overwhelming majority of us have to do all our own lugging. That means we spend a lot more time in our cars. And when we fill them up with gas, we have to do that ourselves too. There always used to be a friendly attendant who not only filled the tank, but also washed the windshield and checked the oil for us.

When men or women no longer do the job they used to, their bosses retire them. But what can we do with whole industries and institutions that don't quite cut the mustard anymore?

Training Your Pet, and Vice Versa

Is it true when people say that after a while dogs and their owners start to look and act alike? My wife and I live with a small Cavalier King Charles Terrier/Poodle mix named Miss Daisy. In dog years, Daisy is about the equivalent of my current age in people years. Apart from our difference in size – she weighs in at about ten pounds and I'm trying to get below 200 – we are becoming disturbingly alike. The worst part seems to be that I'm the one who's changing, not her.

Daisy has always been white. I started out to have blonde hair, then dark brown, and now it's a very poodle-like white. Daisy has always been a voracious eater. I was finicky as a kid, indifferent as a young adult, and now just as eager for a taste treat as my dog. As she gets older, Daisy needs to go outside to relieve herself a lot more often than before. I can identify with that, too. But these are just physical characteristics. It's when I consider personality traits that I especially start to worry about which one of us is influencing the other.

One trait that has long been true of both of us is that we're more verbal than mechanical. I'm convinced Daisy understands nearly everything we say, even the words we spell in her presence (things like "w-a-l-k" and "t-r-e-a-t," for example). On the other hand, in her outdoor restroom, she is always amazed at what happens when she runs full-tilt to the end of her chain's reach. And if she winds her chain around a tree or post, she can't figure out why all of a sudden she seems to be stuck. She thinks it's totally unfair that some unseen force has come along to limit her activities.

It's pretty much the same with me. I can function okay verbally. If my wife gets my attention and speaks slowly, I can usually comprehend her instructions. I can even call up and order food from almost any ethnic group's restaurant. However, mechanical things leave me at a loss. I've made snowblowers conk out, computers crash, cars break down, and appliances give up the ghost. I'm not sure if I was always this way, or if somehow I've succumbed to Daisy's influence.

I always pictured that as a dog owner I would be in a more dominant position. Frankly, it's a little disappointing that I seem to be imitating her instead of the other way around. I must be too suggestible or eager to please. Still, I suppose it could be worse. Years ago, we had a Basset Hound that stole things. Every neighborhood kid's baseball glove ended up on our stoop. If I had followed the example of Gaylord instead of Daisy, I'd probably be in jail now.

To Vitamin Makers, You're a Man, Woman, or Over-55

I was shopping for vitamins the other day and noticed that a popular brand has three different versions of their daily supplement. One is designed for men. One is for women. And one is for people over 55. Wait a minute! Since when did men and women stop being different from each other as soon as they turned 55? Did I sign up for neutering when I signed up for AARP? I have to admit it comes as a shock to learn that sexual differences have disappeared by my age. Here I was thinking those differences were still pretty darn nice. I'm sure this will be big news to certain aging actors and politicians. The people who formulate vitamin supplements are probably all apple-cheeked youngsters. We older folks must seem so alien to them that we all look alike.

Some people used to say that all Chinese looked alike, or all African-Americans, or all nuns. It would be unthinkable to speak that way today – unless you're talking about older people. I guess diversity training can only go so far.

When people think of a truly alien species, what comes to mind? Check out the tabloids in your supermarket. People who claim to have seen space aliens describe them as being grey and sexless. Apparently it's an easy jump to assume that anybody grey is also sexless and a member of some other species (one that has altogether different nutritional needs). So while real men and women get doses of vitamins that presumably enhance and strengthen whatever it is that makes them men and women, we over-55s get some kind of generic stuff whose purpose is just to keep the rocking chair going. After all, only our Urologists care which kind of plumbing we've got.

There could be a more sinister explanation. Maybe the young folks who create vitamin formulas just don't want to imagine sexuality rearing its ugly (or even bald) head among people the age of their parents. Possibly they're still traumatized by having accidentally witnessed a primal scene in their childhood. So they may even be putting something in that over-55 vitamin mixture to prevent anything like that from happening again. I believe I'll go back to the store and check that vitamin label for saltpeter.

Speaking out in Defense of the Modern Cave Man

For the last generation or so, women have gotten into the habit of holding men up to criticism and ridicule. They've made us feel bestial and uncouth because we possess testosterone, because we grow hair where women don't grow hair (or in our later years lack hair where women do have hair), and because we occasionally scratch parts of our bodies that women don't seem to need to scratch. But most of all, they criticize us for how we leave the toilet seat. I think we're getting a bad rap on all counts.

Maybe it's their turn to beat up on us, after a few millennia where the tendency was the other way around. However, in the spirit of balance and fair play, I feel I must rise to defend my gender.

First, let's stop bashing testosterone. It turns out now that both men and women produce it. In fact, some women now take the hormone by doctor's prescription.

We men evolved hair on our faces and bodies to enable us to go out in the cold for necessities like gathering firewood and attending football games. After a certain age, losing the hair on top of our heads is nature's way of telling us it's time to stay inside and watch the game on TV. As for scratching, it's a scientific fact that when skin is covered with hair, it becomes scalp. I'll bet even women scratch dry scalp.

Regarding the biggest issue of all – the position of toilet seats – it's my duty to point out that women don't completely hold the logical high ground. There are two movable components to a modern toilet, the seat and the lid. One possible arrangement is to leave both lid and seat up – which makes the assembly ready for a man to use in the way he most frequently needs to use it. Another arrangement is with the seat down and the lid up. This is the most convenient way for women to use it. The third possible arrangement is with both the lid and seat down. This is certainly the most aesthetically pleasing of the three. It's also the best arrangement ecologically, because it slows the evaporation of water. It prevents your dog from getting the habit of drinking out of the toilet. It prevents your six-year-old child from getting a cold footbath when he needs to step on the toilet seat in the middle of the night to reach the bathroom light. (Okay, that's a traumatic part of my past that may have influenced my feelings in this matter.)

In every way, the seat-and-lid-down arrangement is superior. Is this the way women leave the toilet? No. My research has shown that most women leave it ready for their instant use, with seat down and lid up. How is this different from the attitude of those inconsiderate men who are frowned upon for leaving it in the position most convenient for themselves?

As in many arguments between the sexes, what we're really talking about is not so much what's right or wrong, but merely who generally gets their way. I think if women ever admit that fact, there's a good chance we can learn to live together in harmony someday.

A Modest Proposal for Coping with So Many Seniors

One of the many concerning statistics these days is that people are living so much longer. They say the rising tide of elderly people threatens to swamp the medical care system and bankrupt Social Security. Within a few years, there will be an army of codgers for every struggling wage-earner to support. Pristine Arizona deserts and Florida wetlands will all turn into ugly retirement communities. Too many mall-walking exercisers will drive shoppers away and bring business to a standstill. What can be done about the problem of too many seniors? Well, some HMOs and insurance companies do their bit by skimping on medical care or making it unaffordable for the elderly. The efforts of Dr. Kevorkian a few years ago may also have had some effect. Unfortunately, these methods are just too negative to capture much popular support. What we need is a way to reduce the numbers of old people in a way that's positive – maybe even fun. Here are some suggestions:

My first idea was that seniors should be exempt from speed limits. What could be more enjoyable than cruising along as fast as you like, while highway statistics quietly accomplish the desired social goal? My wife points out a flaw in this approach – seniors might smash into younger drivers, reducing the wrong part of the population. I still think my idea could work if special speed-limit-free senior lanes were added to the freeways. There could even be special highways set aside only for seniors. To enhance the likelihood of accidents, these should be winding, scenic routes through the mountains or along coastlines.

Another possibility would be to encourage seniors to subtract years from their lives by eating rich foods. If you're above a certain age, you should get free meals in gourmet restaurants. Or you could just stay home and have prime ribs and Fettuccine Alfredo delivered at no charge by Meals on Wheels.

Another very effective program would be to require bars to give free drinks to everyone over 62. Signs would read, "No drinks if you were born after (date). Free drinks if you were born before (date)."

To discourage healthful exercise, the city should send someone over to every senior's house to mow the lawn, shovel the driveway, and weed the garden. Free cable TV would also help promote a life of debilitating leisure.

It's rumored that older people sometimes die while having sex. They should be encouraged to have sex as often as possible. Honeymoon resorts and fantasy-suite hotels should offer free weekends for seniors. Romantic cruises should also be given away. These have the added benefit of offering rich buffet banquets at all hours (see suggestion #2 above). In bars, the free drink policy (Suggestion #3) should also apply to any attractive younger person for whom a senior wants to buy a drink.

By investing in these programs, society could eventually save billions in pensions, medical care, and assisted living. Speaking from the standpoint of the seniors, I would have only one question: *Where do I sign up?*

The Ultimate Reality Show

They call it "reality-based television." TV networks love to plunk a bunch of people down in a jungle or desert and force them to deal with a lot of challenges while cameras record every move. Once a week, they have to get rid of one of their members. The last one remaining wins. Hah! Wimpy concept. I've got an idea for a much more challenging and devious TV series. I call it The Aging Game.

We'll start with the usual group of assorted personalities. Our contestants won't have to be isolated on a remote island. We're going to develop even harsher ways to set them apart from the rest of humanity while they continue living right in their own home towns. And the dirty tricks we play on them will be subtler but nastier than any twists that Survivor producers ever came up with.

First, we'll put some kind of drops in their eyes to make their vision blurry. Let's see how they meet the challenge of reading the fine print in their phone book or newspaper. While we're at it, we might as well also fit them with some earplugs to hinder their hearing. Our audience will get a lot of laughs when our contestants try to converse with each other:

"In this sun, a big hat's very wise."

"What? For fun, you dig fat hairy guys? Man, I think you need a shrink!"

"Don't mind if I do. Got any beer?"

The next week, we'll make life even more challenging for our contestants by giving them some injections to make their joints and muscles hurt when they attempt any physical activity. Let's see which ones are brave enough to get up out of their chairs and try to get things done. Hint: It may not be the ones who were the most athletic before. It could be the skinny guy or dainty housewife who copes the best. There are lots of surprises in this phase of the show.

Shows like Survivor and Fear Factor sometimes made people eat awful things they'd never touch otherwise. We won't resort to silly things like bugs and rats. We'll simply tell our contestants that all the food they've enjoyed before is now bad for them. They can no longer eat carbohydrates, fat, salt, or anything that tastes good. Watching them forage in a grocery store or restaurant for sustenance under these rules should be fascinating.

The next surprise we spring on our contestants is really devilish. Those other shows spent a lot of time showing how the people struggled to provide themselves with food and shelter. Usually, all they had to do was catch or pick or dig up something to eat, and slap together a few sticks for a hut. We've got something much more challenging for them.

Our contestants will still have to work at jobs to earn money for their food and shelter. However, they are now required to wear special makeup and wigs that make them look gray and wrinkled.

All the employers in town are in on the game, and avoid hiring or promoting anyone wearing these costumes. In addition, co-workers will be instructed to patronize them. This phase of the competition should see many of our contestants start to crack.

In the next challenge, they're told they can't even work anymore, but must get by on their savings or a tiny monthly stipend. Then they find out they must spend much of that income on medicine and doctors. If they still choose to spend a big portion of their resources on food, shelter, and fun, they may soon realize that this was a painful and unhealthy mistake.

On the other shows, contestants would meet every so often to vote on who has to leave and who gets to stay. The Aging Game is harsher. Your fellow contestants just randomly disappear, and it's usually the ones that everybody liked the best. Nobody ever really figures out how the rules work for this part, which adds to the frustration and tension. Isn't that delicious?

The more I thought about The Aging Game, the more I became convinced that it had real potential. Finally, I pitched the idea to a TV producer. He stared at me with a dumbfounded expression.

"Are you kidding?" he asked. *"We'd be sued by every contestant and fined by the FCC if we treated people that badly! No way!"* I didn't have the heart to tell him The Aging Game isn't actually a game. It's the reality show everybody is slated to star in some day.

You May Get Your Best Results by Using Positive Pessimism

Most people insist optimism is always the best approach to anything. Others find pessimism more realistic. I favor a creative combination of both.

A few years ago, psychiatrists at the Mayo Clinic found that people who scored as optimists on a personality questionnaire in the early 1960s were more likely to be alive decades later. A California study showed that kids who gave optimistic answers on a test 80 years earlier lived an average of two years longer than their more pessimistic classmates. All this confirms what my wife's family has always said. Maintain the right attitude, wear a smile, keep your shoulders back, and everything will turn out all right. My own family, on the other hand, has a long history of believing in Murphy's Law – "If something can go wrong, it will." There is scientific evidence for this belief too. For example, somebody did an experiment years ago that involved flipping pieces of jellied toast onto a carpet. The more expensive the carpet, the more likely the toast would land jelly-side down. I've always been somewhat torn between the viewpoint of my wife's family and that of my own. The optimistic approach should lead to a happier, longer life. On the other hand, how do you square it with the obvious truth of Murphy's Law? The answer is something I call "Positive Pessimism." Optimists visualize something turning out the way they want. Pessimists picture it happening the way they don't want. Those of us who practice Positive Pessimism see it starting out the way we don't want, but then we imagine ourselves handling the situation so wonderfully that we turn the expected bad result into a positive one. This confuses the forces of nature whose job is to make things go wrong, and eventually leads to things happening the right way instead.

Here's an example of how it can work: Back in the mid-1990's, I had a chance to be on Wheel of Fortune. The popular TV show held a contestant tryout at a mall in my hometown of Minneapolis. Hundreds of people were there to compete, and we stood in groups of three to play the game over and over. My pessimistic side told me to expect some sort of problem, and it turned out there eventually was one. After several hours, my bladder felt ready to explode. But if I left to go to the men's room, I'd be out of the game. So I fought on, in the effort to solve puzzles and maybe make the show. In those days, one of the puzzle varieties required you to guess a word and then use it correctly in a sentence. I solved the word "ambivalent." When asked to use it in a sentence, I truthfully said, *"I'm a little ambivalent right now about whether to carry on and take this to the end, or just chuck it all and run to the nearest men's room."*

Well, the woman who was in charge of the contestant search exploded in laughter at that. She even promised that in a couple of minutes we could all take a break. And at the end of the day, I was one of less than two dozen people picked to be on Wheel of Fortune out of the hundreds who tried out. So it turned out that I was right in worrying that something bad was about to happen, but also right in hoping that something good would result.

Positive pessimism also worked for me when I flew out to California to be on the show. This was a pretty big gamble, because we had to pay all our own expenses (and in those days contestants who didn't win a single round ended up with zero dollars, instead of a $1,000 minimum like today). I really needed to win at least enough to cover the travel and hotel.

I could have optimistically visualized myself winning (followed by the usual on-stage jumping up and down and hugging). Or I could have pessimistically pictured myself slinking home in defeat and poverty after losing. Instead, I practiced the art of Positive Pessimism. I pessimistically assumed I would lose every round. Pat Sajac would say something like, *"Well, I'm sorry the Wheel wasn't kinder to you, but..."*

I then optimistically pictured myself replying something so hilarious that Pat Sajac would do a double take and the audience would be convulsed. A long career on the talk show circuit would then open up for me. The more I reflected on this result, the more acceptable the possibility of losing became.

The actual final result had both an upside and a downside. The downside was that I didn't get to come up with a funny reply that led to a career in show business. The upside was that the reason I didn't get to make the funny reply was that I won the Wheel of Fortune bonus round and ended up with almost $50,000 in prizes, minus California and Federal income taxes. I think the lesson positive pessimism teaches us here is that every event will very likely have both an upside and a downside. Even if the upside you hoped for doesn't happen, the downside can possibly yield very favorable results.

Will Pasty or Bruckles Be the Next Food Craze?

In the great American melting pot, ethnic and regional cuisines stayed pretty much within their own cultures until the 1950's. That's when everybody discovered pizza, and then branched out to other Italian dishes like lasagna.

It was just the beginning. With the help of Julia Child, millions then got hooked on French cuisine. Later, Tex-Mex cooking took the country by storm. This was followed by Cantonese, Szechuan, Vietnamese and Thai. Local specialties like Cajun blackened fish and Philadelphia cheese steak spread to every corner of the land.

I keep wondering what the next national cooking craze will be. More specifically, I wonder if any dishes from my own ethnic background will ever hit it big. The only possibilities that come to mind are pasty and bruckles.

The English are definitely not noted for their cuisine, but my Dad's family made great pasty (pronounced PAST-ee). This consists of layers of potatoes (cut as for scalloped potatoes), cubed beef steak, and onions, all baked within a pie crust. It's then slathered with ketchup before eating. Cornish miners carried them to work and kept them warm on steam pipes. My paternal great-grandparents moved from Wisconsin to North Dakota riding in a boxcar with their furniture, sustained by a washtub full of pasties. Other nationalities add things like rutabagas and carrots to their versions of pasty, but the Adams family stoutly rejected these corruptions of their old Cornish recipe. Some Scottish friends told me they love pasty too, but they were horrified to learn we eat it with ketchup. They insist on dousing it with gravy instead. (Well, I don't take the Scottish too seriously about food, since they're the people who invented haggis, a dish supposedly made with such ingredients as sheep's stomach and lamb's heart and lungs.)

On my mother's side (German and Dutch), cooking was designed to sustain big farm families. Nothing fancy. But they had one dish I've never seen anywhere else – bruckles. They made bruckles by pouring pancake batter into a huge fry pan. When the batter set, they would take two knives and slice it into a sort of pancake hash. The bruckle hash was stirred every so often with a pancake turner until done. The original idea must have been to make pancakes for a crowd in a hurry. However, bruckles taste different from pancakes – just as stir-fried chicken tastes different from fried chicken. You can put anything on bruckles that you might put on pancakes, but for some reason they taste best with applesauce. Bruckles are perfect for filling hungry stomachs quickly and at little cost. My mother recalled a childhood friend confiding that during hard times they

Wayne Adams

had bruckles and potatoes every morning and potatoes and bruckles every night.

Of my two family dishes, pasty has come closest to breaking out into the mainstream. Pasty shops can be found in towns that have a lot of miners and quarrymen. Years ago, I visited one in northern Wisconsin. They ducked the ketchup vs. gravy battle by offering both. So far I haven't found bruckles served anywhere except my grandparents' farm, but they deserve a wider audience. I wonder if the Scots would put gravy on them instead of applesauce.

When a TV Survey Calls, Never Tell Your Real Age

When the Caller ID said "unknown name, unknown number," I steeled myself to the task of getting rid of another pesky salesperson wanting to sell me siding or refinance my house. But this call was different – even rather flattering. A survey person was seeking my opinion about TV shows. The woman seemed to quiver with excitement at the prospect of finding out what I thought. Finally, I'd have a chance to influence next season's crop of prime time offerings. The flattery didn't last long. After a few general questions, the interviewer asked my age. I told her. There was a pause.

> *"Is there anyone there between 12 and 39 that I could talk to?"* she asked.

> When I said there wasn't, she replied: *"Well, thank you anyway. Goodbye."*

I was stunned. Age discrimination is usually subtler. Corporations try to make you feel you were actually in the running for that job, but just happened to be narrowly beat out by a younger candidate. The media world seems to have dropped all pretense. In fact, Modern

Maturity reported a while back that we older citizens are not just ignored by the entertainment world. We're the kiss of death. Shows have actually been axed because they were TOO popular with viewers over 50. (Dick Van Dyke's Diagnosis Murder was reportedly one of them.)

When did we become such pariahs to marketers? Doesn't our money spend as well as a younger person's? To paraphrase Shakespeare's Shylock, are we not fed with the same TV dinners, subject to the same coughs and colds, healed by the same patent medicines, warmed and cooled by the same cruises and resorts as they are? If you cut us, do we not apply the same brand of adhesive strips?

Much as it galls me, maybe the answer is to try to "pass" as a young person. Next time a survey calls, I'll pretend to be twenty-something. I'll just happen to be a twenty-something who hates stab-in-the-back "survivor" shows and shallow, off-color comedies. I'll be an unusual new breed of youth who likes dramatic shows with character and plot, comedy shows that produce laughs instead of snickers, and yes, mystery shows where the white-haired old detective figures out who done it.

If enough of us do this, maybe we can throw the marketers into a tizzy over the strange new preferences of the kids they dote on so much. Advertisers and networks may rush to send Jessica Fletcher shuffling on the trail of yet another criminal. Laura Petrie, knitting in her rocking chair, will gush *"Oooooh, Rob!"* once again. And Jeopardy will be back on prime time.

Back when we really were kids, we used to put on our parents' old clothes and play grownup for fun. Now, it may be time for us grownups to pretend we're children. "Let's Pretend" isn't just a kid show any more. Pretending gets more serious – and at the same time more ridiculous – as time goes on. Oh well, doesn't everything?

Modern Barbarians Trying to Mentor Kids

Years ago, my wife and I volunteered a few times to teach a Junior Achievement class at the local grade school. This was a series of five one-hour sessions in a week to teach kids some practical things about how the economy and the world of work function. It was sort of a preparation for being grown up. We started out teaching third graders, and later moved up to fourth grade.

The teaching part wasn't hard, because the Junior Achievement people had all the lessons prepared and organized. What Mickey and I lacked in teaching skills we covered up with a tag-team approach that gave the impression that we were more informed and animated than we really were. And the kids of that age are so enthusiastic it was inspiring just to be around them. That's why I was so ashamed on the day when they saw what a criminal I was.

It was the final session of the year, when it's customary for the Junior Achievement volunteers to bring in some treats for their kids. We had cookies and boxes of fruit juice. In unpacking the juice boxes, I ran into some of that indestructible plastic packaging. Without thinking about it, I pulled out my trusty little Swiss Army Knife to open the bundle. A collective gasp burst from the class. Suddenly I realized that if any of these students had brought such a knife to school it would have meant an automatic suspension under the day's zero-tolerance rules. What they didn't know was that in my other pocket I also had a nail clipper much like one that reportedly had gotten some little girl suspended in another school shortly before. I quickly apologized and tried hard to look less like a desperado.

What a different world twenty-first century kids live in compared to my own school days back at the dawn of time. I hate to admit this, but when I was in first or second grade guys still wore knickers and boots. The coolest boots came equipped on the right side with a little pocket, which closed with a leather strap. In that pocket there was always a jackknife. Yes, we went to school armed to the teeth. Well, armed to about mid-calf anyway. The worst thing any of us ever did with those weapons was to carve our initials into our desks. The schools frowned on this, but I don't recall that anyone ever got suspended over it. Actually, we were probably performing a service. The initials made the school desks more charming and valuable when they were sold in antique stores a few years later.

Now that I think back on the naiveté that accompanied my own formative years, I wonder if those fourth graders I was teaching shouldn't have been the ones teaching **ME** about how to live in the modern world.

Proof of Seniorhood

On the way home from running some errands the other day, I stopped at a drive-in to pick up lunch. I ordered a couple of hamburgers on the machine and then drove up to the window. The cashier's eyes widened with pleasure when she saw me in person. *"Oh, I can do better for you on the price!"* she exclaimed, and proceeded to discount 10% from the total. What a nice surprise, I thought. Was I their zillionth customer? Was it my sex appeal? Did she mistake me for her favorite celebrity? Sadly, no. She went on to say, *"Next time you go through the drive-through, mention that you're entitled to the senior discount."*

Now, I'm quite certain I hadn't mentioned to her that I'm a senior.

There were no AARP decals or Lawrence Welk bumper stickers on my car. On top of that, I wasn't even driving a codger-style sedan that day, but a minivan. I might have been on the way to pick up kids from baseball practice. Yet, somehow she sensed that I'm a senior. I tried every possible way to think of an explanation that didn't involve my looks. Nothing worked. She gave me the discount because I look old. How depressing! The discount was nice, but the way I got it was not.

This raises the question of just how a business SHOULD offer this type of discount. I used to frequent a store that also gave discounts to seniors. They had a sign that said so. But the clerks never offered it unless you asked for it. If you asked, you were old enough; if you didn't ask, you didn't get it. There was no check of IDs, and no evaluation of your appearance. A brazen thirty-year-old could get it, and a shy eighty-year-old could miss out. This method avoids embarrassing the customer, yet it doesn't seem quite right either. Is there some way to give seniors special treatment fairly but without insulting them? Maybe we should look at how it works with other groups.

Take food stamps. When I go through the grocery checkout, the clerk never notices the ratty-looking clothes I often wear and exclaims "Oh, I see that you're needy. I can do better on the price for you." On the other hand, if I told her I was needy I can't imagine her simply taking my word for it. There seems to be a requirement that you actually have some stamps issued by the proper agency. In the same vein, should the Government issue us senior stamps to entitle us to any discount that stores might offer our age group?

Gang members identify themselves with tattoos, lodge members use special handshakes, police officers show badges. What should we seniors use?

In the future, I'll bet we adopt the same system our pets use today. Dogs and cats can have microchips implanted under their skin that could help get them returned home if they're lost. When people catch up to using this technology for themselves, the store clerk will automatically know from your embedded birth date whether you're old enough to buy an R-rated movie ticket, order a cocktail, or get a senior discount on your hamburger. It would be an effective system, but I'm not looking forward to having any electronics placed under my skin. Instead, when somebody asks if I'm a senior, maybe I should just try to learn to stop letting THAT get under my skin. Wait a minute, what am I thinking? I'm a senior (and obviously have the looks to prove it). I'm entitled to be crotchety! That's even better than a discount any day.

Unorganized Fun Is the Real Fun

I think I was born into one of the last unorganized generations. I don't mean DISorganized – although anyone looking at the office in my home would know that I'm a master of total disorganization. I'm talking about UNorganized. My friends and I grew up without the benefit of having our lives scheduled for us. We had no Little League sports teams, I wasn't in the Boy Scouts, and kids in my neighborhood had never heard of summer camp. During the school year, we had to rely on ourselves to find something to do after we got home in the afternoon. And from June until September, we were responsible for the whole day. This wasn't always easy. Countless times I would whine to my mother: *"What's there to DOOOOO?"* She would offer some suggestions, which I would generally turn down, and then she'd give up and tell me to use my imagination.

My friends and I did have some advantages in those days that kids don't have now. The streets weren't yet blacktopped, so every year we could follow and watch the big yellow graders when they came through the neighborhood to dig up and smooth off the dirt roadways and then top them with a fresh coat of oil.

Before everyone had refrigerators, we followed the man who delivered ice to people's houses. He would give us slivers of cool refreshment on hot summer days. And we certainly enjoyed sharing our mothers' garden flowers with the horses that pulled the delivery wagons from local bakeries. (Our mothers, of course, didn't know about that.) Not everything we did was that antiquated. We explored the neighborhood on bikes much as kids do today. We ran around staging mock battles and ambushes with toy guns. We discovered crayfish and exotic bugs along the creek in a park a mile or so away.

The biggest difference between us and the kids of today is that nowadays they never have to ask *"What's there to DOOOO?"* In fact, their little day planners are completely filled with organized activities. Overfilled, I would say.

I used to find a few weeks every summer to stay at my grandparents' 80-acre farm a short train ride from town. When Mickey and I became grandparents ourselves, our grandchildren rarely paid us that sort of visit. Our out-of-town grandchildren seldom could find enough free time for that sort of trip in their booked-up schedules. We didn't even see the grandchildren who lived near us in town as often as we wanted. They were all involved in so many sporting events – baseball, soccer, football, swimming, basketball – the seasons overlapped. The contests seemed very major-league, not only played with spiffy uniforms and padding, but watched over by an amazing number of coaches, referees, and parents.

Now, I guess it's nice for kids to have coaches to help them learn to play the game more skillfully. And referees keep everything going according to the rules. And parents lend support and pride. However, too many times I've seen it turn out badly. At one grandson's football game, the opposing team's grownup followers were so nasty and vociferous that the referee had to warn their head coach that his team would be penalized if he didn't get the adults to behave in a more sportsmanlike way. This is nuts.

Maybe I saw this problem coming way back when I was a kid. At any rate, I avoided taking part in any sports event ruled over by grownups. Well, it did happen once. That was enough. When I was in junior high, a bunch of us were enjoying a pickup baseball game at a local park. One of the kids came up, all wide-eyed and enthusiastic, and said "My dad is a referee, and we could get him to call our game for us!" I thought this was the worst idea ever, but apparently the other kids were in favor. Besides, the man was already walking down the alley toward us, dressed up in his black umpire's costume. It's no coincidence that years later, Darth Vader dressed the same way. All of a sudden we had this guy calling balls and strikes. Previously, we just swung at any pitches we liked. The ones we didn't like simply didn't count. His presence put a lot more pressure on what had been a fun game. The clincher came after I managed to hit a single. I was standing there, a foot or so off of first base like always, when Lord Vader pointed at me and shouted *"Yer out!"* It seems he had a rule that prohibited any leading off. That was the first I'd ever heard of such a thing. After that experience, I avoided as much as possible any activity that involved letting someone bigger than me tell me exactly what I was supposed to do. That sort of thing always stood for drudgery, not fun. In fact, it's probably why I retired early from corporate life and started my own little business.

I can't help but wonder how today's kids will be affected by the super-organized, carefully coached and supervised games they play. Will they grow up to be more motivated to learn skills, follow directions, and pursue goals? Or will they end up like some of the parents and coaches at their games, going totally bonkers when things don't fall their way? Will kids who are used to managing such incredibly full schedules turn into adults who are organized, disciplined, and better able to handle stress? Or will all those years of unrelenting pressure turn them into trembling zombies by the time they grow up? Should I keep encouraging my grandchildren to enjoy all the sports and clubs and educational activities they're signed up for, or should I step forward and tell them about the glorious freedom that comes from spending afternoons and vacations with a minimum of adult interference?

What's a grandpa to DOOOOO?

What Can Replace Our Stock of Obsolete Funny Stuff?

Like most other things in American life, our sense of humor has gone through an enormous change in the last fifty years. Part of this came about because people realized that some things that seemed funny to us shouldn't have. So it's no longer funny to make ethnic or racial jokes. Few people poke fun at religions any more either. So if Paddy and Mike no longer walk into a bar, Ole and Lena aren't married anymore, and that priest, minister, and rabbi seldom walk down the street together, what kinds of jokes are still around? Well, we seniors apparently don't have a strong voice in political correctness circles, so there are still lots of jokes about us. Sex is another subject that remains okay, as long as it doesn't make fun of anyone's orientation. So it stands to reason that jokes about octogenarians attempting to have a sex life are a staple on the Internet.

Aside from political correctness, there's a second reason why much that was funny years ago isn't funny today. A lot of things that were preposterous then are everyday facts of life now. For example, back in the 1980s I once came back from vacation with some samples of unusual beer I'd collected around the country. In those days, stores in my own town carried very few brands of beer, and it was all pretty bland. My idea was to stage a beer-tasting party. These were unheard of at the time. It was supposed to be a humorous send-up of the snobbish wine-tasting parties that some people were starting to hold. My beer-tasting party didn't happen (it turned out that beer deteriorates while riding across country in a very hot car trunk), but I still think it would have been funny – back then.

Today, of course, real beer tasting parties are held all the time, with terribly serious discussions on the merits of the myriad microbrew products now available. So the potential humor in the idea of holding a beer-tasting party is long gone.

Another example: Many years ago, if somebody at a gathering asked me my line of work, I'd sometimes say I was a veterinary chiropractor. You see, that used to be sort of funny because there was no such thing. The idea of spending money on a chiropractor for pets would have been considered ridiculous. Now veterinary chiropractors are all over the place. In fact, besides "traditional" veterinary chiropractors, you can take your pet to specialists in Swedish massage, Rolfing, or Shiatsu. If that doesn't help, you can try someone who specializes in veterinary versions of acupuncture, homeopathic medicine, or other alternative and holistic therapies. No wonder our confused pets have to consult veterinary psychologists more and more often. In my wildest youthful imaginings, I couldn't have come up with a tall tale so far-fetched.

As events continue to make once-ludicrous ideas commonplace, and as political correctness makes once-funny clichés no longer acceptable, how are we going to replace our stock of what's funny? Is it just going to keep disappearing like the rain forest or ozone layer? Or are there new sources we can tap? I think there's hope. After all, elections and politics didn't used to be very funny.

Can Retro People Become as Popular as Retro Cars?

The "old" look is hot right now – unfortunately, not in people but in cars. Not only do you see a lot of carefully restored classic cars on the street, but some of today's models have gone back to the styles of the past: toothy grilles, rounded windows, fancy bumpers, etc. This retro trend in cars is all well and good, but they're missing out on some of the features that made old cars fun.

None of the new retro models seem to have copied the best feature of my first car, a '37 Plymouth coupe. You could crank open the bottom of its windshield for the ultimate in-your-face ventilation. Our '49 Chevrolet had an ignition switch that saved me a lot of trouble. If you turned it off one way, you needed the key to turn it back on. But if you turned it off in the other direction, you could operate it without a key, just by means of a little built-in lever. Back then, my short-term memory apparently was not much better than it is now. After repeatedly locking my keys in the car, I learned to use the key only to unlock the door; then it went right back in my pocket and the ignition was turned on without it. No more locking myself out.

Our '53 Nash had seats that not only reclined, but folded down into beds in case you were overcome by drowsiness, or perhaps affection, while driving. (I know what you're thinking, but we were old married folks with a child by the time we owned that one.)

Some of the best features of the old cars will probably never be possible to bring back. Take their radios. Oh, they couldn't play FM stations and weren't powerful enough to be heard ten blocks away like today's car radios. But they played better music and carried actual entertainment instead of just irritating talk-show hosts endlessly taking calls from dull listeners.

The other thing they'll never recapture is the price. My first used car cost $75, the second one was double that at $150, the third one came in at about $300, and the price-doubling trend has definitely continued to this very day. If I don't get out of this pattern, a few cars from now I'll be paying what the whole GM factory was worth when I started out. On the whole, though, I have to applaud the retro trend. If it spreads from cars to people, maybe even a 1934-model Adams could be in demand someday.

We Should Let Car Makers Know What We're Really Looking For

Our car is beautiful and fun to drive, but it's got over 175,000 miles on it, and it may soon be time to look for a replacement. I'm not at all sure I'm ready to deal with the super-intelligent cars of today. Not only do today's cars cost more than twice what our first house did in 1960 ($14,775 brand new), but they also contain more computing power than the entire Pentagon did that same year. I suppose it's nice to have a car keep me informed about the direction I'm going, the temperature outside, and how many miles before I run out of fuel. But I don't really need to know many of the things the new cars want to tell me, such as my average speed since buying the car and the total number of gallons of gas I've pushed through it. And I don't need door locks that can be programmed six different ways.

One of those programs features a several-second delay between the time you close the door and the time the car locks itself. The idea is that this gives you the opportunity to slap your forehead, say "Duh!" and open the door again to pick up whatever you forgot. This may sometimes be helpful, but I think it's rather patronizing on the part of a car.

When I turn off the ignition on one of these smart cars, the radio keeps playing on the assumption that I must be entertained until the last minute. But as soon as I open the door, it will turn the radio off lest I forget. Again, patronizing.

If the car is so concerned about my memory, it should worry about whether I remember to make the payments or renew the insurance. So far as I know, cars don't yet step forward responsibly to check on those details.

All of these new features in smart cars are very perplexing to a guy who is still not convinced that today's automatic choke is as reliable as the old manual choke was. Now cars come with computer screens that can connect you to the Internet. In addition to delivering e-mail and supplying route directions, they can direct you to the nearest sushi bar or doughnut shop. Once again, this seems to be a feature I could live without.

What sort of car is most enjoyable? I remember the time we took a couple of grandchildren to a go-kart track. Now, there's a simple vehicle. A gas pedal and a brake pedal, that's it. Yet, people flock to drive them, not because they need to get someplace but just because they're so much fun. Maybe car makers should incorporate a little go-kart simplicity into their products.

They need to realize that guys love cars mostly for their looks and fun, not their brains. Sorry, gals, if that's a bit like our taste in women too, but I'm afraid guys tend to be guys.

Let's Shop for Dumber Appliances!

In the previous bit, I mentioned my misgivings about the high intelligence of the new cars being sold today. Now it sounds like within the next few years all our home appliances will not only be very smart, but they'll be talking to each other. It's enough to give a person the shivers.

They say your TV will be able to tell you if you've left the refrigerator door open. Now, I happen to think that my TV and refrigerator already dominate my life more than is healthy. When they start getting together, I may not have a shred of independence left. If the TV broadcasts a commercial for beer, will the refrigerator automatically open its door and pop the lid on a can? Will the refrigerator eject a doughnut whenever the detective on a cop show stops for a snack? How will I convince my wife that my diet and I were innocent victims of an electronic conspiracy?

Future refrigerators will also be able to keep track of their contents and alert you when you're out of something. I suppose they will do this through the TV again, or through a flat computer screen built into their door. Maybe they will just dial up some cybergrocery store and order a new supply. I picture myself trying a new brand of peanut butter, hating it, but then being locked into buying it the rest of my life simply because the refrigerator keeps reordering it.

When I was a kid, ice boxes interfaced with the outside world, not through TVs and modems, but through print media. When they ran out of ice, homeowners would put a card in the window telling the ice man how many pounds to deliver. I hope people back then appreciated how that system made them an important part of the decision-making process. If for some reason they chose not to put the card in the window, the ice box stayed empty.

When electric refrigerators came in, they could guzzle all the power they wanted without their owners' by-your-leave. I think that was when we started to lose control of our daily lives.

Houses are developing the ability to unlock the doors when your kids come home from school, turn the heat up or down, and adjust the water temperature – all by remote control from a computer. If that electronic home operates anything like my computer, after a few months it will probably start to hang up or crash every so often. Your TV will needlessly warn you that your refrigerator is dangerously low on resources. Your refrigerator door's computer screen will say "Access denied" when you try to get a glass of milk. The water heater will flash "fatal error" when you are about to step into a hot shower. The only solution to these things might be in much the same way you handle your computer problems – by shutting off the house's main circuit breaker, going outside, and then coming back in to start over completely.

If things get so out of control that you try to flee, don't expect much help from your car. It'll probably be in league with the rest of them.

Franklin's Folly

In many ways, Ben Franklin was one of the most inspiring Americans ever. Starting out in poverty as a runaway apprentice, he became a great businessman, diplomat, patriot, and probably the most prolific inventor since Leonardo da Vinci.

Yet there seems to be no public celebration of his birthday on

January 17th. Maybe the reason is that we're holding his one big screw-up against him. It's hard not to. One of his inventions has caused endless frustration and trouble for me and, I'm sure, for millions of others. No, it's not his invention of the lightning rod that I'm referring to. Oh, it's possible that a few people may have been electrocuted trying to copy his experiment that involved flying a kite in a thunderstorm, but he had warned against that. His lightning rods are altogether good things, and have probably saved many buildings from burning down.

Nor is it his Franklin Stove that I object to. Heating homes with metal stoves instead of open-hearth fires saved lots of fuel and also made houses less likely to burn down. His interest in home fires also led him to start the first volunteer fire department and the first fire insurance company. No problem for me there either. After he was appointed postmaster, he invented the odometer and attached one to his carriage to help him plan postal routes. Although the odometer reading on our aging car causes me considerable concern, I really can't fault Franklin for that.

His invention of swim fins, an improved version of a musical instrument called the glass harmonica, or watertight bulkheads for ships don't bother me in the least. A simple invention of his called the "long arm" consisted of a pole with a grabber on the end to pluck books off the top shelf of his library. When I was a kid, every neighborhood mom and pop grocery store had one to help the shopkeeper reach items on the upper shelves. All good.

Some people are discomfited by urinary catheters, which he invented to help his brother deal with kidney stones. Luckily, they're a device that so far I haven't had to make use of. Painful as they may be, I'm inclined to think they do somewhat more good than harm.

No, there's really only one invention of his that I wish he'd never thought of: bifocals. The story goes that he got tired of switching back and forth between his regular glasses and reading glasses, so he combined the two lenses in one set of frames. On the face of it, this must have seemed like a good idea – UNLESS HE ACTUALLY TOOK THE TIME TO TRY THEM!

I have to assume Ben Franklin lived in a one-story house, because if he had tried walking down a flight of stairs in his new bifocals he would have tossed them in the wastebasket right away. I also believe that if he had looked at the dashboard of his carriage to check his other invention, the odometer, he would have realized that it was too far away for the lower lenses in his bifocals and too close for the top ones. He also must have had somebody else read the newspaper to him, or he would have suffered a perpetual crick in his neck from tilting his head up to read.

What was the man thinking? And what were all of us thinking who came after him and allowed ourselves to be persuaded to wear these things? How did somebody talk my dad, who was otherwise

a very intelligent man, into wearing an even worse variation – trifocals? It's a mystery how he could see anything at all through those kaleidoscopes. I sure can't claim to be any more sensible than all the others who succumbed to Franklin's silly invention. I also wore bifocals for many years, until cataract surgery in both eyes gave me new lenses.

In general, Ben Franklin was a great guy. But I guess even geniuses can make a major goof at least once in their lives.

If It's Overly Gourmet, It Came from Out West

First it was wine, then beer, now coffee and even water. Just about all the liquids that pass our lips are getting way too complicated. And a lot of it can be blamed on the West.

Things used to be so much simpler when I was young. If my folks decided to celebrate a holiday with a small glass of wine at dinner, there were only two choices: Manischevits and Temple Kosher. And we weren't even Jewish. Back in the 1940s and 50s, our neighborhood liquor stores in Minnesota didn't carry any other brands. Both of those sweet red wines came from New York State.

Later, folks on the West Coast began to dominate the growing of wine grapes. All of a sudden, there were a lot more choices of wine in our local stores. With the expanded interest, wines imported from Europe also became commonly available. Soon, a lot of people began to work hard at developing – and talking about – their immense knowledge of how the subtle differences in wine affected their discriminating palates. You started hearing about bouquets and nuances and hints of various kinds of foliage. It was a whole new language.

Now, I've always enjoyed a glass of wine as much as anybody, but I've sure never considered myself a wine expert. In fact, I thought some of the more snobbish aspects of their obsession were really pretty ridiculous. Soon, gourmets even began staging beer tasting parties, a funny trend that started in the western part of the country too!

The next drink to be adopted by snobs was coffee. Now, I thought I knew about coffee. I had been drinking it since I was in grade school, when I spent part of each summer on my grandparents' farm. While there, I copied the example of my uncle, who was just a year and a half older than me. He hated milk, since there was no refrigeration on the farm in those days and therefore any milk you drank was as warm as when it came out of the cow. He preferred coffee, so that's what I drank too.

My grandmother's coffee was just a standard store-bought grind. She brewed it early in the morning, and it sat simmering (and strengthening) on the wood stove until you got around to drinking it. Although it had a great deal of authority, I don't think it had any particularly subtle nuances (and I wouldn't have been capable of noticing them if it did). In fact, none of that sort of thing really happened to coffee until after Seattle-based Starbucks began promoting the idea in the 1970s that coffee was worth a higher price if it was sufficiently special. Now coffee connoisseurs expound on fragrance, aroma, flavor, aftertaste, and body. And like wine, specialty coffees now come with suggested food pairings. Pul-eez!

It's even happening to water. People argue about which brand of fancy bottled water is best. Again, this seems to have started out West where it first became fashionable to walk around with a supply of water attached to your belt.

Do you begin to see a trend here? We had wine, beer, coffee, and water in the East and Midwest all along, but none of those things had snob appeal until that was imported from the West Coast.

If you doubt my theory, look at tea. The British and Bostonians have enjoyed tea for ages, and even know the difference between Darjeeling, Assam, Oolong, and Earl Gray. But their enjoyment didn't graduate into obsession. I haven't seen a bunch of newspaper columns on tea, or tea tasting clubs conducting elaborate tests, or a Tea Spectator magazine publishing crucial ratings. I think it's because the West Coast doesn't seem to have gotten into tea very much as yet.

How about ice cream? My choices as a kid were pretty much limited to vanilla, chocolate, and strawberry. Later, Ben and Jerry's popularized the notion that you could have hundreds of flavors. And yet, being from the East Coast, their product never became the obsession of overly-serious gourmet groups.

Why are people from out West so much more concerned about these things? Maybe it's something they inherited from their ancestors. Traveling in a covered wagon, you needed to be an expert in deciding whether a spring or stream was potable or poisonous. If you were good at it, you were more likely to survive and contribute to the gene pool. All well and good. But my Minnesota-based gene pool is a little different. Our Scandinavian and German pioneers had allowed railroad companies and other big real estate operators to sell them farms in a land covered by snow most of the year. That experience led them to teach their children to distrust and resist any idea that was presented to them by slick outsiders. The lesson has served their descendants pretty well. Today, we tend to apply that attitude to self-proclaimed experts trying to impose their hoity-toity ideas on us.

I don't know how this conflict will end. But just to stand up for my heritage, I'm now going to have some cheap coffee made with ordinary tap water, followed by a dinner accompanied by some box-wine that is tasty but totally without pedigree. A votre sante!

Old Is the New Black

Regardless of how they may have voted, back when Barack Obama was elected most Americans approved the fact that his success was a sign of America's having moved beyond the days of racial discrimination. Our country became closer to treating all people with equality and respect. Now if only we can manage to achieve that kind of progress in the way we treat one more group – seniors.

We still have a long way to go. In fact, seniors are in some ways at about the same stage African-Americans were half a century ago. You'd have to be at least my age to remember when help-wanted ads in the South would say "whites only" or "colored may apply." Those days are long gone, but today's employers still routinely take age into consideration when hiring and promoting. Sure, there are laws that say they're not supposed to practice age discrimination, but everybody does. Today's Walmart greeter is sort of the equivalent of yesterday's Pullman Car porter. They're smiling, friendly, and working at the only job they could get.

More and more seniors these days are also living in segregated housing. Apartment buildings, neighborhoods, even whole towns are springing up for our kind. As you might imagine, people who are not in our group wouldn't be caught dead living there. Sound anything like that other segregated housing issue our country used to have?

Although restaurants generally let seniors in, they do try to get us to dine early so as not to bother their normal customers. Some of them also want us to order off a special seniors' menu, where the portions are smaller and selections limited.

If you want to rent a car, you'll pay more if you're over 70, and you may not be able to rent one at all if you're over 80. How long has it been since businesses could discriminate so blatantly based on race? But age discrimination seems to be okay.

And what happens if you're driving a car and have some kind of stupid accident like crashing through a store window? The newspaper account won't mention your race or nationality. But if you're over a certain age, you can be absolutely sure the story will read that "an elderly man drove his car through the window of a store on Main Street." So the media are against us too.

Maybe the ultimate way to end discrimination against seniors is to achieve something on the order of what Barack Obama did for African Americans and see if we can get an older person elected President. Oh wait, I guess that's been tried already.

When I talk to younger people about age discrimination, they always insist that THEY have no prejudice against senior citizens. Then I spring the acid test: "Would you want your daughter to marry one?" Case closed. I just hope we can learn from our black brethren and solve our discrimination problem in something less than half a century from now.

Does Your Wish-List Say That You're from Generation T (For Toys) or C (For Clothes)?

The type of gifts you want for Christmas or your birthday aren't always the type you're given. When I was a little kid, all I ever wanted was toys – Lincoln Logs, Tinkertoys, train sets, toy soldiers. Clothing was never on my list. But older people often seemed to have the idea that clothing was a better gift for me – especially warm stuff like mittens, sweaters, and pajamas.

As a teenager, the toys on my wish list changed to bike accessories, books, and records. What older people thought I wanted was more likely to be things like trousers, tee shirts, and sneakers. When I became a husband and father, my preferred toys included power tools, the latest audio or photographic gadgetry, and anything to do with cars. By this time, generations both younger and older felt that what I really needed were ties, dress shirts, and loafers.

Now that I'm officially a senior citizen, my list of toys includes computer software and hardware, books and magazines, or theater tickets. Younger generations, aware that we senior citizens have thinning blood, tend to bring us full circle by getting us the warm fuzzy mittens, sweaters, and jammies of our childhood. It's not that I didn't need or appreciate every gift of clothing my loved ones gave me over the years. In fact, I'm sure they were essential for me. Being color blind and having no fashion sense, I have always needed all the help I can get in building a wardrobe. Besides, for the last fifteen years I have sensibly put off buying any clothing myself because I've been trying (not very successfully) to diet away a lot of pounds. If it weren't for gifts, I guess I literally wouldn't have anything to wear.

So I'm not complaining about usually getting clothing as gifts. But I'm extremely surprised at the way youngsters today now look upon the whole toys-versus-clothing issue.

Today, all of our grandchildren tend to have nothing but clothing on their Christmas lists. These lists seem to be in the kids' own handwriting and not coerced by their parents. I think that's an astonishing change from how it was when I was their age. Maybe part of the reason is that our grandkids recognize that many toys today come with a mortgage instead of just gift wrap. The latest video game console or tap-dancing robot doll is a major investment. As for the kind of toys that most grownups like – boats, motorcycles, snowmobiles – well, forget it unless you've won the lottery.

My wife, being a year younger than I am, has a foot in both my generation and the next one. She has a balanced Christmas list – toys like my generation and clothing like one of the younger generations. She tells me about all the items on her list that are in the toy category, such as mixers or toasters. Usually these come with a specific make or model number to help me understand. Her clothing list, which requires some taste plus understanding of sizes and colors, she entrusts to our kids.

I suppose I could just be overlooking the obvious. Maybe there is really no great difference between the generations over whether we prefer toys or clothing on our wish list. Or maybe the answer is just that some of us never quite made the transition to the present day.

Men Are from Pluto, Women Are from Saturn

To understand the relationship between men and women, you have to realize that they belong to different planets. No, not Mars and Venus, like you usually hear. Those two aren't all that different from earth. It seems obvious that men and women are so different from each other that they must have come from places that are very different too. I believe there is strong evidence that men are from Pluto and women are from Saturn. Now, to understand this you have to think of the planet Pluto as not being named for the god of the dead and ruler of the underworld. You have to think of it as being named for the cartoon dog. Eager, sloppy, none-too-bright. Like a dog being walked on a long leash, Pluto ranges back and forth. Sometimes it's the ninth planet from the sun, sometimes it swings inside Neptune's orbit and lopes along as the eighth planet.

As for Saturn, you have to think of it as being named not for the Roman god of agriculture, but for the car. Shiny. Beautiful. And of course, when a car comes along, a dog can't resist the impulse to chase it. He has little chance of catching it and no chance of controlling it if he does catch it, but chase it he must. If you look at Saturn through a telescope, you see why someone would be attracted. It's the most beautiful planet. No doubt that's why it's surrounded by so many followers (18 moons at last count, more than any other planet). And then, of course, it flaunts those gorgeous rings. Yes, Saturn is definitely feminine.

Shaped by Our Stars

To see how this theory applies to humans, I only have to look as far as my own family. My wife, Mickey, and I have three sons and three daughters. I'm pretty sure this is a big enough sampling for a survey. If not, Mickey says it's as big a sample as she intends to provide. All three of our sons married their high-school sweethearts. It was *"Nice to meet you. I love you. Here, all I have to give you is my freedom. Please take it now!"*

On the other hand, our three daughters dated a lot of suitors. In fact, each was engaged twice before finally settling down to marriage. It was more like: *"Hello there. Ho, hum, maybe you'll do. We'll see."*

Why is there this difference? Why must males pursue with single-minded instinct, while females coolly calculate their choices? Why do bucks find it necessary to bash their heads against each other while the doe calmly says, "You boys work this out; I'll be having lunch in the clearing over there"? Why did knights gallop headlong with lances pointed at each other's hearts just to impress ladies who sat in the bleachers calmly eating bon-bons?

I think it's for the same reason a puppy will cheerfully put himself through any amount of exercise and indignity just to hear his mistress say *"Good boy!"* It's our Plutonian heritage. That's not to say that women find their Saturnian background entirely a bed of roses. While we're slaves to our need for a single-minded quest, they can never forget that they're surrounded by choices. It's what compels them to pause and touch every object made of cloth as they walk through a department store. In their own closets, (with just a slightly smaller selection than the store) they can't choose what to wear quickly enough to actually go someplace on time. And when they do manage to arrive at a restaurant, it's all they can do to solve the menu in time to have dinner.

Transcending Our Instincts

It seems to me that both men and women would benefit if we could tone down these differences. We would lead more balanced lives, reach more of a common understanding, and avoid many of the dumb things we do. If it were just a matter of testosterone and estrogen, the process would be simple. A pill or shot could take care of it. Overcoming our planetary origins is harder. Here are some exercises that might help:

At a restaurant: if you're a man, try saying *"Hmmm, what to have, what to have…"* When ordering a drink, make sure it contains at least five ingredients and comes in several different varieties (strawberry, banana, and so on). If you're a woman, say *"Just burn me the biggest steak you've got!"* Drinks must never contain more than one or two ingredients.

Shopping: If you're a man, force yourself to look for a new outfit even if you haven't completely worn out your old one. Make a game out of looking at more than one before buying. If you're a woman, don't go shopping at all unless forced. When you do shop, stay within a fifteen-minute time limit.

At the movies: If you're a woman, throw yourself into the experience of a movie consisting of just one continuous chase scene. If you're a man, cultivate a liking for films exploring complex relationships and emotions. If nothing really happens in the movie and you feel sad afterwards, give yourself extra credit.

At work: If you're a woman, get out there in front of the pack and chase that sale or sign that deal before anybody else does. Beat the pants off your competition so you can take over the company. If you're a man, concentrate on resolving a myriad of complex issues with the other members of your team. Use intrigue to get everyone on your side so you can take over the company.

On a first date: Come to think of it, there really are no exercises that will help here. No matter how much we try to change ourselves, men are still going to be from Pluto and women from Saturn. We might as well accept it. It's written in the stars.

Baldness Bashing Is Over!

From the time I was in fourth grade until I was 70 years old, I never received any compliments on my hair. In fact, from my thirties through my sixties, good-natured insults were the norm. Then an attractive woman stood on stage and singled out my bald head from an audience of hundreds of people, actually praising its absence of hair. Well, it changed my whole outlook! In fact, her insight cast a new light on the already shiny subject of baldness.

As a toddler, I had long, blonde, curly hair. Honest, there are pictures to prove it. By the fourth grade, my hair was slightly less blonde but was still, as I look back, fairly gorgeous. Then my mother gave me 35¢ (the price of a haircut back then) and sent me to the neighborhood barber by myself. Do I hear a gasp? No, my mother was not neglectful. In those days, it was okay for moms to let their kids walk around town alone. The dangers that now stalk children at every turn had not been invented yet. In fact, I generally walked to the corner grocery to pick up something for her more than once a day. (Back then, the store owner recognized you and wrote down your purchase in a little book and your parents paid for it at the end of the week.)

Anyway, when I came home from the barbershop that day I announced (although I didn't really need to): *"I got a heinie!"* Another thing you should know is that in those days a heinie was not the posterior part of your anatomy, but a very short haircut. I think the name referred to the sort of hairdo favored for many years by German soldiers. Even in those World War II days, political correctness had not yet changed the name to "crew cut." All my friends were getting heinies, so naturally I thought I should too.

My mother was devastated by the loss of my curls. What's more, like other forms of lost innocence, they never came back. My hair remained straight when I later adopted the longer style with the wave in front that was eventually copied by the Fonz, Richie Cunningham, and Elvis Presley.

Shortly after high school, two of my friends started losing their hair. One responded with an ever-more-elaborate combover, while the other cut his hair short and went defiantly bald. I thought his choice looked much better. So when my own hair started leaving in my late twenties, I embraced this new look that nature had decreed for me.

From that time until now, I've accepted the way I look. Still, I can't say it's the way I would have chosen. Other people tend to be amused by baldness, even though they wouldn't make fun of you if you had some other defect. I think the problem is that, down deep, society thinks a man should have hair where women have hair – and only there. If he lacks hair on his head, he's old and decrepit. Hair on his face and chest and back, however, means he's rather bestial and uncouth. Consequently, we have men wearing wigs to make up for the lack of hair on their heads and scrupulously shaving to counter the growth of hair on their faces. It's like having a low-grade sex change operation every day in an effort to conform to the standards of a matriarchal society.

I figure that hair grows where it wants to, and I'm okay with that. As a result, I've probably saved a lot of money on razor blades and implants over the years. But I always felt in the minority regarding my views on hair – at least until that on-stage compliment I mentioned above.

It happened at an Erma Bombeck Writers' Conference in Dayton, Ohio. One of the keynote speakers that year was author and columnist Patricia Wynn Brown. She also produced Hair Theatre, a one-woman show that explained much of the human condition through attitudes toward hair. A cancer survivor herself, she donated proceeds from Hair Theatre to buy wigs for women and girls who needed them after chemotherapy. At a reception the night before her speech, she went around asking people for their personal hair stories. I shared my experience trading my curls for a heinie, and she mentioned it in her presentation the next day.

Then she singled me out in the audience. *"You'll notice that Wayne is a REAL MAN!"* she said. "Baldness, of course, is caused by having plenty of testosterone." And she congratulated me for what everybody else had been teasing me about for all those years. I think I could have saved the price of an airline ticket and flown home just on that remark.

Let's Split Up the Olympics

My wife and I avidly watch both the Summer and Winter Olympics on TV every year that they're on. Of course, we each like different events and for different reasons. Maybe that's why the Olympics are so fascinating. They're a living example of the things that both unite and divide the human race.

The portion of the Olympics that I like best (such as track and field, volleyball, and weight lifting) comes under the heading of sports. The part she likes best (gymnastics, diving, figure skating, ice dancing, skateboarding and so on) is really theatre. To me, the judging controversies that happen in those contests are a blight on the whole affair. Was this gymnast unfairly penalized, should that diver have received more points? The complicated scoring business turns me off. On the other hand, I have a feeling my wife thinks that's the most fascinating part.

I guess I must be just an old fogey, but to me Olympic events should conform to the Olympic motto: "Citius, Altius, Fortius" – swifter, higher, stronger. Whoever gets to the finish line first, jumps the highest, lifts the heaviest weight, or makes the most goals is the winner. There's nothing in that motto that mentions doing it so gracefully that the judges give you a lot of points on some arbitrary scoring system. Performing in such a way as to please a set of "expert" critics is the province of the theatrical and artistic world, not sports. It's not that I don't enjoy watching gymnasts, divers, and figure skaters perform. I'm hugely impressed by their feats of grace and strength. I just don't think that what they do should be regarded as sports simply because there's physical activity involved. There's physical activity involved in strip-tease dancing too, but nobody suggests that it should be included in the Olympics (well, nobody except possibly me).

In my opinion, any event that cannot be judged by some objective standard such as a stop watch, tape measure, or number of goals, should be taken out of the Olympics. That's not to say we should eliminate those events, however. We simply need to transfer them to the realm of theatre, where the judgement of critics is the norm. So let's have two separate venues. We can still call the sports one The Olympics, named for Mount Olympus (home of the Greek gods, who didn't seem get all that involved with the idea of conforming to elaborate standards). Those other events that must be graded by judges we could call The Sinais (for Mount Sinai, where God handed Moses the most famous set of standards).

But separating the two kinds of events doesn't completely solve things for me. It would be nice if we could recognize the best gymnasts, divers, and figure skaters without going through those painful controversies that always seem to come from an opinionated set of international judges. Once we recognize that this stuff is theatre, not sport, we just may be able to come up with an answer.

In the theatrical world there are plenty of self-appointed critics who rate performances. However, the public is free to ignore them. We can choose a different winner by voting with our pocketbooks. Whether it's your favorite country star, opera singer, big band, or symphony orchestra, which ticket you buy is entirely up to you, not up to some critic's judgement.

Maybe instead of a formal competition with a solemn set of judges, the gymnastics and diving worlds could put together something like the Cirque du Soleil, a traveling circus featuring spectacular exhibitions by top performers. The organizers would, in a sense, vote with THEIR pocketbooks by hiring the performers who attract the biggest crowds. The competition would simply take the form of an audition, where giving a pleasing performance would be more important than whether you took an extra half step after that dismount. Participants would therefore be encouraged to take more chances and do more spectacular stunts.

There are ice skating shows that already do something of the sort, often with performers from the Winter Olympics. Unfortunately, I believe some of them still retain the judging structure from the Olympics. If they left that part out, I would enjoy the show even more, like in the good old days of the Ice Follies. But then, that's just me. Maybe it's a guy thing.

On the other hand, my wife is more tuned in to the subtle nuances of evaluating somebody's actions. She understands and appreciates the complicated processes involved. Believe me, she really digs evaluating. It must be a gal thing. Mind you, I'm not saying for a minute that gals tend to be, um . . . judgmental. Let me reiterate and emphasize that point while leaning over backwards to stress it as strongly as I can. I'd also advise all you guys to adopt that stance. Let's just say that gals tend to identify with activities that invite careful evaluation and taste, whereas guys prefer results that are immediate and obvious. Sort of the way gals are more likely to be discriminating foodies and guys are a bit more into simple guzzling.

So if we do split the Olympics into two camps with very different approaches, we'll just be making them conform to the way the rest of the world seems to work already. What do you think?

"My Name Is Wayne Adams and I Disapprove of These Messages"

Are you as sick of negative political advertising as I am? How I long for the good old days when political campaigns were more positive and polite. Advertising consisted mainly of buttons and lawn signs. Neither of those had enough room to mount much of a personal attack on the other person running.

Campaigning consisted of actual live speeches by the candidates – not sound bites oversimplifying their own positions or misrepresenting the other person's. And the speeches tended to be more gentlemanly (sorry, but politics is sometimes most accurately described by politically incorrect terms).

I remember my parents being very offended by what they called Thomas E. Dewey's "mudslinging" when running against Roosevelt in 1944. I was too young then to pay attention to whatever Dewey said, but I'm sure it was very mild compared with the acid barbs candidates hurl at each other today.

Political advertising changed when the media folks began persuading political parties that perception is reality. What a terrific deal that is for a candidate! No need to actually have better ideas and the will to follow through with them. All you have to do is seize on some slogan or issue, harp on it enough, and if people buy it you win.

Product advertising, too, was much better in the old days when all advertisers followed an unwritten law of civility that forbade even mentioning the competition. You could praise your own toothpaste or vacuum cleaner as long as you didn't put down somebody else's product. That went out of style several decades ago. There was actually quite a shock when the first commercial – I think it was a car ad – mentioned a competitor in a negative way.

Mild comparisons then began to be tolerated in product advertising. In political ads, these eventually turned into nasty slurs. They seem to keep getting worse in every election. Now our radios and TVs threaten to poison the very air in our living rooms.

And yet, the solution could be so simple. Political candidates are a lot like pharmaceutical companies. They're both trying to peddle nostrums that they say will cure whatever problems we have.

So how do the rules say that drug companies must advertise? After every magazine ad for a medicine, there's a lot of fine print that explains and largely contradicts the claims made in the ad. On radio or TV, a narrator with a toneless high-speed voice provides the fine print as part of the ad.

I think political ads should be required to follow the example set by the drug companies. What would the fine print contain? Let's follow the model for drug ads and include the following:

1. A thorough explanation of all claims. If the ad said *"I successfully fought to reduce taxes,"* the fine print would say something like: *"After pressure from groups of my supporters and with the cooperation of some of my enemies, I voted for a bill that lowered the tax by 5% on telephone bills for those people who have two or more beige-colored phones."* Any negative claims would require very careful documentation: "When we say that Senator Jones beats his wife, we are referring to their frequent games of Gin Rummy, which he wins 61% of the time."

2. Possible side effects. *"Voting for me may lead to a frequent need to pay higher taxes related to my uncontrollable itch to spend."*

3. Contraindications. *"You should not vote for me if you are – or are likely to become – handicapped, unemployed, retired, or a college student."*

4. Harmful interactions. *"If you elect me President and at the same time elect a majority of the other party to the House and Senate, four years of severe paralysis may result."*

Think about it. When we take a prescription, we don't decide on our own what drugs are safe and effective for us. Our doctor does that for us. And yet, drug companies are required to give us all that fine-print qualification anyway. With elections, we have to make the choice ourselves based on whatever data we have. So isn't it ten times as important for politicians to provide the same kind of honest detail that drug companies do?

Come to think of it, this is too good an idea to use only in advertising. How about this: whenever a candidate gives a speech, a "translator" stands off to the side reciting those toneless high-speed fine-print words that explain the real truth of the matter.

The only disadvantage I see in this approach is that the TV networks could suddenly lose an awful lot of advertising revenue. And maybe there would be a shortage of candidates running for office. I think I could live with that.

New Phones Are a Tough Call

I can remember telephones that only grownups could use. Now we have phones that only kids can use. Once again I have to ask myself – when did the world turn upside down?

The "grownup" phones were big wooden boxes with cranks on the side, mounted so high on the wall that they were above the reach of most youngsters. The "kid" phones are the new cellular ones, so tricked up with electronic programs that hardly anybody my age can figure out how to work them. My acquaintance with the old-style wooden phone dates back to one that hung in my aunt's farmhouse when I was about eight years old. It was a party line, so there was a code of long and short rings that signaled whether an incoming call was for you or someone else. Of course, many folks on the party line picked up the phone on every call, just to hear all the news.

The first phone I remember in my parents' house was one of those skinny candlestick models about a foot tall. This was followed by several round and then square desktop phones, which in turn were replaced by those streamlined Princess phones. Their last phone was a big square wall model with oversized numbers to accommodate my mother's poor eyesight.

My wife and I now have a portable home phone with a viewing screen that helpfully divulges details of who's calling or on hold, the last numbers we've called, the time and date, and lots of other stuff we may or may not want to know. My problems aren't so much with that one, but with our cell phones. They're well-intentioned, but just so complicated!

For example, I'm fully aware that cell phones can take pictures, but this has never happened on mine. Quite possibly it never will. Mickey takes countless photos on her phone and shares them with friends and family, but I still prefer to use an old-fashioned camera for that.

I've never sent text messages with my phone either. Texting has to be a lot more work than simply talking to somebody, right? Besides, I understand you have to learn an entirely new language. To me, LOL means to relax in a chair, not laugh out loud.

Whatever you want a cell phone to do these days, it always seems "there's an app for that." Mickey's "smart phone" does it all. My own cell phone, an ancient one that actually deserves the title "dumb phone," doesn't do so well, although it's capable of a lot more than I know how to make it do.

For example, my phone can keep track of my calendar as well as the names, addresses, and phone numbers of everybody I know. In my one venture into the high-tech world, I used to synchronize this information on the phone with the same program on my computer. Recently, however, my phone and computer seem to have had a spat. They no longer talk to each other. Who knew these little machines could develop such strong emotions?

I'm not willing to take the time to enter all this stuff twice. So now I have to print out a calendar and stick it on the refrigerator, just like in the old days. My cell phone is back to simply making calls.

I guess I'm just not ready for the art of today's telephony. These modern marvels in communication are wonderful, but I'm not sure I'm ready to take the plunge into the latest technology. First, it would be a mammoth learning process (and guys my age know that mammoths can be quite frightening when riled up). Besides, I'm a little nostalgic about the old forms of communication that are disappearing. Like writing letters. Or walking down the sidewalk saying hello to people sitting on their front porches.

I guess I'm going to have to ask my grandchildren for some training. They seem to be experts on everything electronic. Maybe, in exchange, I could regale them with stories about how people used to be able to turn a crank on the side of a wooden box and then talk to a live human being who would then plug in a wire to connect them with their friends. I'm sure the kids will find it just as mysterious as today's technology looks to me.

Another Technology Bites the Dust

I can't believe it's already happening again. A once-popular piece of technology is starting to disappear. This is getting to be too much of a habit these days. Oh, bits and pieces of technology have always tended to go away. Whale-oil lamps. Horse-powered streetcars. Crystal-set radios. But this whole process has really sped up during my lifetime.

Some of you may remember handwritten letters. It was a very personal way of thanking your grandma for a birthday gift, expressing your love to a sweetheart, or staying in touch with old friends. It's pretty much a lost art now. In a related development, kids no longer slip crumpled notes to each other in school. It's all done by texting now.

Newspapers are becoming another relic of the past. When I was a boy, it would have been unthinkable not to subscribe to a daily paper. Many people got both the morning and afternoon editions. Now all newspapers are losing circulation and I worry they may not be long for this world.

The kind of radio programming that existed when I was a boy died out long ago. Back then, many radio stations put on entertaining local shows with live studio audiences, accompanied by a house band or at least someone who played the Wurlitzer. Later, stations switched to simply playing recorded music, which was much cheaper to broadcast although there were still some ASCAP fees involved. More recently, a lot of them have switched to talk radio. As you no doubt have heard, talk is cheap. In fact, it's free. That's usually about what it's worth.

And when it comes to talk in their own lives, more and more people now are even doing without home telephones. They get along instead with just their cell phones or Internet-based phones.

Now, even a technology that I thought was almost new is showing signs of fading away. I'm referring to email. A while back, I sent an email to a grandson and granddaughter. I expected them to read it right away and respond soon after. Instead, they still hadn't even seen it a week later. Why? Because now they do all their corresponding on social networking sites like Facebook. Old fashioned email is so passé! Why, it dates all the way back to the 1970's and 80's, even though most of us never got acquainted with it until around the turn of the century. Wait a minute – turn of the century? That sounds really ancient too.

I've got a theory about why all these technologies are biting the dust. Writing letters started becoming less popular when mailboxes started bulging with junk mail. Newspaper pages became mostly ads and very little news. Radio programs turned into almost endless commercials. Sales calls overwhelmed our home phones. And of course, spam now fills our email inboxes. Too much advertising takes away the fun from any technology.

We've got to figure out how to keep this from happening to the technological marvels we still have left. The only way to make them stay useful, fun, and popular is to keep advertisers from dominating them. Unfortunately, I don't think there's an app for that.

Email, iphones, PDAs,
are among the things we're gonna lose
if salesmen don't stop finding ways
to make 'em maddening to use.

A Toast to the Gentler Sax

Something terrible has happened to the saxophone. I'd love to be able to hear again the melodious saxes of "String of Pearls," the haunting saxes of "Harlem Nocturne," or even the cloying saxes of "The Waltz You Saved for Me." Time was, when you wanted a sure-fire piece of music to put your date in a romantic mood, you were safe in requesting "anything with a saxophone." Now, any other instrument — even a tuba or base drum — might be better.

The saxophone world is dominated today by screeching soprano instruments. They sound like clarinets with PMS. What's more, they're usually fuzzed up electronically to enhance their ability to put your teeth on edge. Melodically, fingernails on a chalkboard are preferable. Where did these things come from? Did foreign terrorists build them in secret laboratories and release them in this country to spread like a virus? Or are they simply a botched attempt to invent a better civil-defense siren?

The first time I noticed the dominance of screechy saxes was on "Saturday Night Live" back during its heyday. Well okay, they seemed to fit with the edgy tone of that show. Unfortunately, that kind of sax apparently fit in all too well with today's high-tension world. Soon, they became a requirement in any kind of music that doesn't consist entirely of drums and guitars. One radio station that advertised "smooth jazz" played mostly screechy saxophone music — as smooth as a crosscut saw. They're off the air now.

I wonder whatever happened to all the tenor and baritone saxes. They probably hang on the walls of fern bars along with old gas pumps and beer signs. They're quaint mementos of the past, just like those of us who loved to listen to them. The situation calls for strong action. First, all of us who remember what saxes used to sound like should mount a rescue operation. Check pawn shops, the walls of trendy bars, and antique malls for old non-screechy saxes. Next, contact any genuine sax players who are left. Pour over your high school yearbooks for those gangly band members with the receding chins who used to play reed instruments. Ask music stores to look through their archives for historical arrangements. Finally, to bring it all together, we may have to rent time in secret paramilitary camps. I picture it like Ray Bradbury's "Fahrenheit 451," where book-lovers got together in secret to preserve the best parts of their culture. In a camp in the mountains of Montana, accountants and telemarketers will practice old Glen Miller arrangements. In the Arizona desert, attorneys and construction workers will pour their souls into incredibly romantic solos. They'll carefully pass on these skills to their children and disciples. Then someday, let us hope, real saxophones can come out of hiding. A new generation will discover what it's like to hear this instrument without wincing in pain. And young people will be surprised to find that "anything with a sax" will put them in the mood for love, not war.

My Generation's Secrets for a Happy Marriage

When people who've known us for just a short time learn that we've been married for well over 60 years, they almost always ask, "What's your secret for staying married so long?" Our family members, as well as those friends who've known us for many years, never ask. It wouldn't occur to our family to ask, because kids just naturally expect that their parents will always be together. Our old friends don't need to ask because they started out the same way we did. We all came of age in the days when it was infinitely easier to form lasting relationships than it is today. You got married young and stayed married. That was how life worked. Times are a lot tougher for couples today. For example:

Economics
The 1950s were a time when opportunities were high and expectations

were low. The slogan in those days was "two can live as cheaply as one," so people got married soon after high school. Homes were very modest and affordable. Nobody felt the need for expensive motorized toys. A couple actually could live on one income. Although women were still discriminated against in the work force, they did have more opportunities than they'd had in the past.

We got married at the end of my junior year in college. When we left for our honeymoon, I had just over $30 in my pocket. Believe it or not, that bought us lodging, meals, and gas for a three-day trip! That's all the time we could take anyway, because I had to find a summer job as soon as we got back. The thing was, I was pretty certain I'd find one. That was in the days before American jobs had started to move overseas. During my senior year, between my part-time work and my wife's job, we managed to pay all our bills (including our $50 a month rent and my $425 per year tuition at a private college).

Today, couples face astronomical mortgages and the need to keep up with the Joneses while worrying about the permanence of their jobs. If they're college students like I was, they probably pay well over $15,000 a year in tuition. That's a lot of stress to overcome in a marriage.

Culture

When we were kids, the movie stars we looked up to were Roy Rogers and Gene Autry, our singers were Bing Crosby and Perry Como, our comedians were Bob Hope, Jack Benny, and Fibber McGee. All of them married for life. The celebrities that youngsters are familiar with today get married and divorced so often the weekly tabloids have trouble keeping up. How are kids supposed to know that this isn't really how it should work?

History

Although people in my generation married young, we generally knew our spouses for quite a while beforehand. We had walked them home from school, escorted them to the prom, and been interrogated by their parents (who were probably acquainted with our own parents). Even before we sorted out into couples, we knew each other as friends. Yet, although we had known each other for years, we married young enough so that we weren't yet set in our ways. We were still flexible enough to grow our attitudes and opinions with each other's help. So most of our history, both before and after marriage, we built together.

Nowadays, even though people are older when they marry, they usually lack the benefit of that long history together. They meet in bars or on the Internet, often without any interrogation or approval on the part of their parents. After they marry, they discover they have irreconcilably different views on politics, food, entertainment, or wall coverings, and the marriage is soon headed for the rocks.

Another thing: With many couples today, chances are that they did not escort each other on that first journey of discovery into the wonders of love. That important bit of history likely happened long ago and with somebody else. They lack a shared intimate milestone that would help keep them devoted to each other for life.

And reason number one... All the things I mentioned above are factors that may help explain why our marriage made it to more than 60 years while so many other ones don't. But I saved the most important reason for last. I had an unfair advantage. I somehow managed to snag the most loving, loyal, beautiful, and exciting woman in the world. Tough luck, all you other guys!

Just When Did I Lose Control?

I seem to be the first guy in my family to lack control over the things that I own, whether animate or inanimate. My grandpa was the complete boss of everything on his 80-acre farm. During my extended visits each summer, I saw that the horses obeyed his every command perfectly. The cows came down the lane right on schedule each afternoon (how could they tell the time?), and each one walked directly to her assigned stall in the barn. The chickens gave up their eggs willingly to my grandparents (although they pecked angrily at me whenever I was sent out to collect their treasure).

The farm had no electricity but there was a lot of equipment, from the horse-drawn plows and wagons to the gasoline-fired pump that filled the stock-watering tank. Grandpa could make it all work perfectly with a little tinkering. Everything he owned seemed bent to his will.

My dad was somewhat the same way. The dogs and cats we had over the years always seemed obedient to him. When something in the house broke down, he could fix it even though the results weren't always aesthetically pleasing. As far as I could see, all the machines in his workshop did pretty much what he wanted them to.

Not so for me. Animals and machines all seem intent on dominating me instead of doing what I want. My car tells ME when I should change its oil or have the engine checked or make a turn or even close the door. I'd get rid of it, but I understand that the new ones are even bossier! My computers sometimes have the nerve to tell me "access denied" when I try to open a file. I paid for you – how dare you talk to me that way! My old laptop was the worst. Several years ago, I connected to the Internet with it from a hotel room. In the process, the computer apparently developed feelings for that hotel. Afterwards, I had to type in the password, "guest," every time I turned it on. I'm your owner, not your guest, you jerk!

As for animals, it's our little dog, Miss Daisy, who tells me when I should take her for a walk, fill her dish, or hold her on my lap. If only my grandpa had taught me how to exert more control!

Miracle Substance Found, You'll Never Guess Where

Just when I had gotten used to the idea that medical news is always bad, I ran across a happy discovery. For a change, science didn't uncover some new disease that's caused by eating one of my favorite foods. Nobody found that the air I breathe or the water I drink contains some previously unknown poison. Nobody announced that the very act of breathing causes some sort of repetitive motion syndrome. Instead, I read that some years back a group of scientists discovered that human fat is a valuable, life-giving treasure. What news could be more glorious? I'm sitting on a fortune – literally.

A couple of doctors, Marc Hedrick from UCLA and Adam Katz from the University of Pittsburgh, had reported that cells found in human fat could be turned into a variety of other tissue types. In laboratory dishes, the doctors were able to coax plain old fat (obtained by liposuction) to grow into healthy muscle, cartilage, and bone cells. Fat holds the promise of eventually being able to regrow all sorts of body parts.

Up until then, people thought only stem cells obtained from aborted embryos and fetuses could do that. Needless to say, research involving stem cells derived from unborn humans draws intense opposition on moral grounds. So far as I'm aware, nobody has voiced any moral objection to sacrificing fat cells in the name of science.

So what we have here is a substance that people always looked down on, but that may turn out to be the key to curing many of the diseases and injuries that plague mankind, while providing a solution to one of the big ethical controversies of our time. Doesn't that make it seem like fat has been unjustly maligned? The portly gentlemen and zaftig matrons who monopolize the buffet line may turn out to be your best hope for the future. I can see the day when the Red Cross Fatmobile will come to your neighborhood to take vitally needed liposuction donations. After you give, instead of just cookies and juice they'll probably offer you a cheeseburger and fries. At a time when America's trade deficit keeps growing, the coming worldwide demand for fat could help tip the balance back in our favor. Statistics on obesity say that we lead the world in production of this commodity. What Saudi Arabia is to oil, we'll be to fat cells.

Another beautiful thing about fat is that it's a renewable resource. No mining, no refining, not even any fertilizer or herbicides are needed to keep the supply coming. The boom in fat will help people of all classes. Wealthy industrialists will be inspired to donate frequently to Red Cross fat drives in order to take a hefty tax deduction for their rich restaurant meals. Families of modest means will be able to start their own little cottage industries growing and selling fat to supplement their income.

To celebrate this brave new world, why not take a fat person to lunch? As a matter of fact, I'm available tomorrow.

Mother Nature's Laws Change with the Years

I used to think that Mother Nature's laws were universal and permanent. Now I realize how much they change as you go through life. We already know that time is relative. Albert Einstein, one of my contemporaries (in history, not occupation) told us that many years ago. I don't know what effect that fact has on a galactic scale, but I do know what it does to people. When you're in grade school, the time between the tardy bell and recess stretches on for a century. But when you get to my age, one birthday is succeeded by the next in the blink of an eye.

Let's take a look at another natural law – gravity. We've all pretty much accepted the rule, "What goes up must come down." It works on such things as baseball pop flies and erupting geysers. But when it comes to people the rule seems to break down if you're above a certain age. Things like blood pressure and cholesterol just keep going up and up, as does the price of the pills designed to keep them from doing so.

There are also other ways in which gravity discriminates depending on your age. When you're a kid, gravity is your friend. It powers sleds, roller coasters, and playground slides. But once you're past middle age, gravity begins to turn on you. You can't lift as much or jump as high. What's worse, parts of your body begin to sag inexorably downward through that ever-more-powerful force.

It would be nice if we could get a university or foundation to fund some research into what makes the laws of nature change over the years. I've written to several, but nobody seems very interested.

I've got a theory of my own. What are we really looking at here? Mother Nature is suddenly exhibiting some odd mood swings. She's also apparently having hot flashes, in the form of global warming. I think we all know what usually causes these symptoms. Mother Nature has apparently reached middle age. Maybe we could try hormone replacement therapy for her by replanting the rain forest or something. Otherwise, we can just be patient and wait a few years until things settle down. I'm confident that, as with most of us, the older she gets the more she'll mellow out.

Then and Now

For those of us who came of age in the 50s and 60s, some terms we often heard back then may sound like terms we hear today but that have very different meanings now. It's important to pay attention to the changes. Some examples:

Then: Try buying some killer weed.
Now: Try spreading some weed killer.

Then: Getting out to a new, hip joint.
Now: Getting a new hip joint.

Then: Moving to California because it's cool.
Now: Moving to California because it's warm.

Then: Being called into the principal's office.
Now: Storming into the principal's office.

Then: Peace Sign.
Now: Mercedes Logo.

Then: Planning to get your head stoned.
Now: Planning your headstone.

Then: Long hair.
Now: Longing for hair.

Then: Acid rock.
Now: Acid reflux.

Then: The perfect high.
Now: The perfect high-yield mutual fund.

Then: Do a keg.
Now: Do an EKG.

Then: Swallowing acid.
Now: Swallowing antacid.

Then: pothead.
Now: potbelly.

Then: Watching John Glenn's
historic flight on the news with your parents.

Now: Watching John Glenn's historic flight
on the History Channel with your kids.

Then: Trying to look like 50's movie stars.
Now: Trying not to look like 50's movie stars.

Then: Hoping to pass the driving test to get your license.
Now: Hoping to pass the vision test to keep your license.

Then: Popping pills & smoking joints.
Now: Popping joints.

It's Not Just the Climate That's Warming

One of the nicest benefits of aging is that our relationship with everyone else becomes warmer. Yes, pretty much everyone. When you're in school, you do have friends but basically you're all competing with each other, whether it's for grades or in sports. And there may be a bully who makes recess scary and a crabby teacher who makes the classroom unpleasant.

The rivalry picks up when you enter the world of work. Again, you have friends but there's a great deal of competition for sales, promotions, and achievement.

When raising children, your loving relationship is tempered by the need to teach and control them.

Finally, when you've retired from work and your children are grown up, you can totally enjoy life and everyone in it. No need to compete or control. All that's needed is warmth and companionship. Relationships should be a hundred times more fun. Bask in the glow. You've earned it.

Part Two:
Why the World Needs Seniors

*Though we don't get a lot of respect
it's not just a matter of vanity
to point out the wondrous effect
that seniors have had on humanity*

Elders Should Be Thanked for Inventing This

"It's raining, it's pouring, the old man is snoring," we used to sing when we were kids. Now that I'm sort of in the "old man" category myself, I take a much less disdainful attitude toward snoring. In fact, I'm beginning to see it as a vital part of the human story.

My snoring was recently compared to the roaring of a lion. I never hear it at all, of course, since I'm sound asleep when it supposedly happens. But my wife never hears it either. What's that? You say she has simply gotten used to it over the last 60-some years? Okay, here's the topper. Our granddaughter, who once shared a bedroom with us for ten days while on vacation, slept right through it too. On the other hand, our son and daughter-in-law, whom the three of us were visiting, actually bought ear plugs for the occasion. They were also the source of the "lion's roar" description.

There seems to be a distinct difference between the generations in their ability to hear snoring. Why do you suppose that is? A scientist would probably say that humans acquired that trait because it conveys some sort of evolutionary advantage.

I'm guessing that back when people lived in caves and were employed as hunter-gatherers, we elder members of the tribe had to do our bit to help protect the group. We were no longer mighty with spears and clubs, but in time we learned to mimic the sound of lions in our sleep to scare away potential enemies. The young adults in the tribe were programmed to stay awake when they heard us, because they were needed for sentry duty. Youngsters, having no defensive jobs, developed the ability to ignore our snoring and get their beauty sleep. There would have been another benefit to the tribe. Young adults who were kept awake by the elders' snoring were likely to produce more offspring. Needless to say, this was helped by the tendency of the tribe's youngsters to sleep peacefully through our snoring.

So when you think about it, snoring actually developed as a vital part of human life. Those of us who still practice this ancient art aren't out to annoy you. We're preserving our heritage.

It was probably a prehistoric man who invented the wheel, and as a result men are still obsessed with wheels today. And ever since some early woman invented weaving, women can't get their hands on enough clothing. Well, we seniors are entitled to remain enthusiastic about our own special invention, the snore. And I'm sure my wife would be quick to point out that if the snoring of elders really helps nudge young adults into getting busy with procreation, certain grandchildren can expect more visits from us in the near future.

The Grandfather Hypothesis

Grandmothers are now getting much of the credit for all the progress ever made by the human race. Well, that assumption has been popular in our family for years, but the idea is spreading throughout the scientific community too. Anthropologists call it the "Grandmother Hypothesis." It seems that humans are the only species whose females live a long time after their reproductive years. Even long-lived animals like elephants and whales keep having young all their lives. We humans came to dominate the world because our ancestors invented menopause and consequently developed grandmotherhood as a career. This freed older women from the dangers and duties of childbearing so that they were available to help nurture their grandchildren, forage for food, and share their wisdom with the tribe.

By studying teeth from ancient skulls, Anthropologist Rachel Caspari from the University of Michigan traced what proportion of our predecessors, over the millennia, lived to be well past the age of sexual maturity. The numbers gradually rose from the days of the Australopithecines through the early Homo Sapiens and Neanderthals. Then, 30,000 years ago, the proportion of older folks suddenly shot up. This coincided with the rapid flowering of human culture at that same time. Dr. Caspari inferred that the older population, particularly post-menopausal women, set off a cultural revolution. The development of language, tool-making abilities, and social bonding are all credited to grandmothers.

That's all well and good. Lord knows, grandmothers certainly deserve a lot of credit. But I feel like asking Dr. Caspari what she thinks grandfathers were doing all that time. Maybe we had a little bit to do with building civilization too. For example, I think it must have been an early grandfather who figured out how to combine two simple tools – the inclined plane and the lever – to invent the first recliner. Primitive codgers were now able to comfortably keep an eye on things in the cave. This freed grandmothers to forage for roots, young men to hunt game, and young women to take the kids to the park. While guarding the cave, those early grandfathers undoubtedly traded stories about their youthful hunting exploits, much as we enjoy doing today. Since language was still in its infancy, they illustrated the walls of the cave with pictures of the game they had vanquished. Thus they originated art.

In order to see these cave paintings better, early grandfathers had to figure out how to tame fire and bring it inside in portable form as torches. Then they made some of the greatest discoveries of all. As the various grandfathers sat there boasting of their past hunting days, they enlisted the help of young boys to carry torches over to light up the spot on the cave wall where their particular illustrations were located. Since language was still being developed, they signaled these young helpers by slapping their hands together.

Thus we see that it was grandfathers who not only invented recliners and action pictures on the living room wall, but also devised remote ways to select which of those pictures to show – even an early version of the Clapper. I think these achievements actually eclipse their later invention of the wheel. That was necessitated by the need to build carts to haul around their heavy primitive golf clubs made from rocks lashed to sticks.

So I think it's time somebody came up with a Grandfather Hypothesis. We were there too, folks!

Understanding That No Problem Is So Urgent That You Can't Put It Off

In his book, Tom Brokaw called my parents' contemporaries who fought World War II the "Greatest Generation." Then there's my kids' generation, which may be the most affluent one of all time. Their kids are the most technically advanced ever. I keep looking for a claim to fame for my own generation – some ability we've developed to its fullest. I think it's this: No matter how urgent or important the problems that beset us, we have the ability to put off deciding on the solution.

At first glance, this might seem like a bad thing. It means, for example, that we have delegated to some future generation the responsibility for fixing Social Security and the environment and crime. Presumably it will be a generation that has both the cash and the smarts to know what to do. This is not a dereliction of our duty. This is a wise recognition that we don't yet have the answers to these problems – and a demonstration of our faith that mankind will continue to grow in intelligence over the years.

Actually, it's something of a breakthrough to realize that it's better to do nothing than to do something stupid. The great horrors of history happened when people were mistakenly convinced they had the correct and final answer to something that was bothering them. NOT having the answer leaves us free to come up with creative ways of postponing a decision. To show how this can work, let's take a look at some very thorny dilemma – say, capital punishment. On the one hand, taking the life of a murderer makes the punishment fit the crime. It brings "closure" to the victim's family. It may also serve to deter other potential murderers. On the other hand, if taking a life is evil, what does that say about the authorities who practice capital punishment? And what if, after the execution, it turns out the convicted person was innocent?

The first step is to admit that we're not smart enough today to answer questions like this. The next step is to look for a satisfying way to put off the decision.

As it turns out, one has been right in front of us for years – cryogenics. And this is a solution that my generation can take credit for, because cryogenics as we know it today got its start in the 1960's. Nowadays, people can choose to have their bodies frozen just after death in hopes that future scientists will find a cure for the disease that killed them. (Future scientists will also have to discover how to bring them back to life, but no doubt that's just another technicality.) So instead of giving condemned criminals lethal injections, why not simply freeze them? If later evidence proves them innocent, we thaw them out. *("Sorry about that, Sam. By the way, meet your 87-year-old grandson.")* As for the guilty ones, we can deal with them way off in the future when people finally figure out the ethics of capital punishment. *("Bad news, Louie. We woke you up because you get the chair tonight.")*

With a little thought, the biggest problems of our time can all be dealt with. Not solved, but dealt with. All we have to do is send them off to the future. I'm sure our descendants will appreciate our showing so much confidence in them.

How Seniors Can Help Baby Boomers Prepare

Now that the Baby Boomer generation is entering seniorhood, perhaps those of us who have already made the transition should help them adjust. It's very important that Boomers do this right, because (due to their sheer numbers) their concerns, needs, and values have always dominated the rest of us.

When the Boomers were pampered kids, we went through a flurry of school construction and TV puppet show development. When they discovered puberty, we went through the sexual revolution (as though it was all a new invention!). When they got jobs and learned about making money, materialism ruled the land. Now, poor things, they're approaching retirement. All of a sudden it seems like the biggest public concern is saving Social Security and dealing with the high cost of prescription drugs.

Those of us who have already reached 65 could tell the Boomers how to deal with this next stage of their lives. It isn't as big a deal as they're making it. There's just one simple principle to remember. When you're older, everything will be more or less the opposite of what it was when you were a kid. For example, when you're younger, if you don't watch your diet your face breaks out. When you're older, if you don't watch your diet your hips bulge out. In general, as your age goes higher everything happening on your body goes lower.

When the Baby Boomers were teens, Customs agents paid special attention to young people entering the country on suspicion that they might be bringing in illegal drugs. Now, they guard against seniors bringing in cut-price prescriptions. The profiling works pretty much the same, except now they focus on tour buses instead of VW buses.

When you're a teenager, your parents suspect that you're sexually active. When you're a senior, your kids are certain that you're not. (One more example showing that parents tend to be right more often than kids.)

When you're starting out your career, the business world is ruled by stodgy old guys who look on younger workers with condescension. When you're winding up your career, the business world is ruled by arrogant whiz kids who patronize their elders. (You can identify with the power elite by practicing stodginess when you start out and arrogance toward the end – while bucking the trend by being condescending to your elders and patronizing to the youngsters.)

Magazines aimed at teenagers are filled with ads for lotions, potions, and fashions that guarantee to make them more attractive. Magazines aimed at seniors are filled with ads for adjustable beds, foam shoe inserts, and pain relievers offering some hope of comfort. The truth is that most teenagers need to be more comfortable with their lives and many of us seniors could stand to pay more attention to our appearance. Maybe we should trade magazines.

When you're a teenager, you worry about passing the road test so you can get your driver's license. When you're a senior, you worry about passing the eye test so you can keep that same license.

If the Boomers prepare now to face these flip-flops, the world might be spared the turmoil that always seems to come when they lurch from one stage in life to the next.

You Don't Need to Be Strong to Be Tough

I've never been what I would call a tough person. I was timid in sports as a boy. As a parent, I was squeamish about bandaging cuts and pulling out slivers. My grandparents, now THEY were tough.

When I was a boy, every summer I used to visit the 80-acre farm where they had managed to support ten kids. Grandpa, a wiry 120 pounds soaking wet, could outwork any three ordinary men. Grandma helped with the milking, raised a huge garden, cooked on a wood stove, and hauled water from a hand-operated pump. Grandma's washing machine was a wooden tub with an agitator she worked by pulling a lever back and forth by hand. Then she wrung the clothes through a series of washtubs before hanging them on the line. She did all this with chronic back pain. Her housedress always had a big hole in the back from her constantly rubbing the sore spot. That's toughness.

My parents were pretty tough too. In talking about the old days, my dad said "Your mother was one of the great ones. When I was ready to give up during the Depression, she'd tell me *'We'll make it! We'll make it!'* When I was out of work, she'd bundle you up and take you on the streetcar to go and do housework. I always told her she had more courage than a Prussian sergeant."

My Dad delivered fuel oil back then, when he could find work. During World War II, volunteering to teach first aid for the Red Cross got him interested in science. His Red Cross supervisor helped him get a menial job washing test tubes in the University of Minnesota's Physiology Department. Over the years, he worked his way up to become chief administrator and assistant to the department head. He contributed to the pioneering heart research done at the University in those days and was listed as co-author on a few papers. Sometimes, while Physiology Department professors gave a lecture, my dad helped illustrate it by expertly running tubes through a research dog that was lying in front of an X-ray machine. It was quite an achievement for a former truck driver with a high school education.

At times it seems as if each generation of my family is a little softer than the one before. I'm certainly not as tough as my parents and grandparents. Our kids had it easier than my wife and I did, and our grandkids and great-grandkids probably have it the cushiest of all. Is the human race evolving toughness out? What makes someone tough enough to overcome hardships, make sacrifices, or fight for their country? Do you have to grow a thick skin and become hardened to life? No. We ordinary wusses can grow tough. We simply have to love life and each other enough to do whatever's necessary.

We May Still Make Mistakes, but They're Not as Serious

People seem to constantly make fun of seniors when they catch us making mistakes: little things like forgetting someone's name, or where we left our glasses, or the route to the shopping center. I think we should try to put a stop to this constant criticism. One possible way might be to point out that the mistakes seniors make are incredibly minor compared with the big mistakes that younger people make – things like bad educational or career choices that lead to dead-end jobs, having or causing unwanted pregnancies, hanging out with the wrong friends who might get you in trouble with the law.

Obviously, we seniors must have gotten smarter over the years if the kind of mistakes we make today are so much less harmful than the ones younger people tend to make. The younger generation needs to understand this. One way to do it would be to confess to them the terrible things we did back when we were their age. That way they'd understand how maturity has made us smarter, not just forgetful. So tell your kids, grandkids, and younger friends about all the really awful, stupid choices you made in your early days. Then they'll realize how much smarter you've become now. It should really impress them. Tell you what – you try it and let me know how it works.

Those Who Worked at Lost Arts Are Cultural Treasures

Our government has a program to list and protect historic buildings. But in Japan, they go us one better. They include people too. Japanese artists and groups who are skilled in traditional arts or crafts can be designated as Intangible Cultural Assets. The really important artistic gurus are further honored with the title Living National Treasures. They get a lifetime pension and financial aid for training their disciples. This kind of support goes to people who practice such things as calligraphy, porcelain painting, stylized forms of theater, and ancient kinds of music that are in danger of dying out.

Of course, if we began a similar program in this country, we'd have to adapt it to our own culture. We've never had a lot of people doing calligraphy, porcelain painting, or inscrutable opera. America's talents have been more in the realm of business. But there are plenty of once-vital business skills that are in danger of disappearing.

For example, companies used to have people who operated the billing machines that were needed to make a business go. Since they were paid on a piecework basis, they developed typing speeds that were incredible to watch. They kept this up hour after hour, with never a sign of carpal tunnel syndrome. Where are they now?

There are other lost business arts. I used to see folks from Accounting on their way to the "computing" room. One would have his arms loaded with boxes of punched cards. This was the data. The other would be carrying a heavy plug board, about two feet square and covered with hundreds of little wires. This was the program. The board went into the side of an IBM collating machine and told it what to do with the information from the cards. There was a lot of skill involved both in punching the cards and in wiring up the plug boards – skills that probably have disappeared today.

There's a lost art that I once practiced myself. Multi-image slide shows were a big part of many corporate meetings. On a very primitive computer, we would synchronize 16 to 20 slide projectors, a movie projector, various lights, and other equipment to a sound track. The result could be an overwhelming wide-screen spectacle. Video projectors and shrinking corporate budgets spelled the end of it all.

My favorite practitioners of lost business arts are the people who ran the early manual calculators known as Comptometers. When entering numbers, their fingers simply flew. Instead of reaching all the way up to the 8 key, they often would just hit 4 twice. To multiply 1,573 by 25, they would simultaneously hit the 1,5,7, and 3 keys (in the right four columns) five times, then move a column to the left and hit the same numbers twice more. There were unbelievably complex ways an expert could get the machines to subtract, divide, and do square roots.

I think some of the people who operated billing and keypunch machines or who wired plug boards and programmed slide shows should be designated Intangible Cultural Assets. But the Comptometer operators are the ones who probably deserve to be the Living National Treasures of American business.

A Lesson We Should Learn from Elisha Gray

During the years when I toiled in a corporate cubicle, I had one man's name – Elisha Gray – written on a 3 x 5 card tacked above my desk. For some strange reason, nobody ever asked who he was. Although he lived before my time, Elisha Gray was important to me. I had learned a big lesson from him.

Elisha was born in 1835 in Barnesville, Ohio. He was a smart, hard-working guy. Forced to leave school early when his father died, he later put himself through prep school and two years at Oberlin College while supporting himself as a carpenter. At college, he got interested in electricity, and soon patented an improved telegraph relay. He went on to patent around 70 other inventions, and founded the company that became Western Electric. But that's not why I kept his name in front of me every day. Elisha Gray is sort of the patron saint of two groups I belong to – procrastinators and people who habitually *"missed it by that much,"* as Maxwell Smart used to say. On February 14, 1876, Elisha Gray went to the Patent Office to register his newest invention, the telephone. The only trouble was that an hour or two earlier, a guy named Alexander Graham Bell had filed for a patent on the telephone.

It turned out later that Gray's version was actually better, and would have worked the way he described it in his filing. Bell's telephone wouldn't have worked the way he had it on his original designs. Nevertheless, after years of court battles, Bell won out as the owner of the patent on the telephone. That's why we didn't end up with a Gray Telephone Company, later broken down into a bunch of "Baby Grays."

You have to wonder how Elisha Gray spent those couple of hours that made all the difference. Maybe he enjoyed a leisurely breakfast, relishing the day that he thought would be his crowning achievement. Maybe he shopped for a new suit that would reflect his imminent financial success. Since it was Valentine's Day, he may have stopped to buy some candy for his wife or sweetheart. Since it was America's centennial year, he may have taken some time to plan how to work his new invention into the celebrations coming up in July. Or he may have devoted a couple of hours to making last-minute improvements on his invention – perhaps the very changes that resulted in it being superior to Bell's (not that it ended up mattering).

There are always pressing little tasks that take us away from the really urgent thing we should concentrate on. For example, a few decades ago I decided to read a lot more magazines in order to help my chances of winning the Publishers Clearinghouse Sweepstakes. Instead, I should have spent my time developing this great idea I had for a TV series about business apprentices competing with each other for success and trying to avoid being fired by a host who would later become President. Too late now. (Okay, I didn't really come up with that TV idea.)

To avoid the dangers of procrastination, it's very important for each of us to remember the example of Elisha Gray. In fact, one of these days when I get around to it I'm going to put his name up again above my desk here at home.

Seniors Have Better Vision Than Youngsters

Just because they see us fumbling for our glasses to read a newspaper (or holding it out at arm's length), young folks often foolishly say we have vision problems. Nothing could be further from the truth. Oh, we may have eyesight problems. But eyesight and vision are two different things.

Today's society is obsessed with sights, not vision. On the evening news, the anchor can show us every natural disaster and human atrocity in colorful clarity. The weather person can show us the tiniest clouds that may be heading our way. The sportscaster can show us, over and over, a close-up of a spectacular play. These are, to be sure, amazing sights gathered by an energetic host of reporters and photographers. But vision requires a longer view. And that's something we seniors are better at.

I must have been prematurely old, because this idea began to impress itself on me way back when I had just finished my sophomore year in college. The year was 1954. At about 5:00 a.m. on June 30th, I stood with my future wife and mother-in-law on a hillside in Minneapolis to watch a total eclipse of the sun. As we progressed through the stages leading up to the total eclipse, we took all the precautions we were told to. Instead of looking directly at the sun, we projected an image of it onto a sheet of paper. Finally, the total eclipse came. Then we could turn and look directly at this remarkable sight.

Now, whenever you see pictures of a total eclipse in a newspaper or on TV, you always see a close-up view. It's interesting. The black orb of the moon covers all of the sun except for flares of the sun's energy marking a ring around the outside. But those closeup views today, like the ones that I saw in the newspaper back in 1954, can't begin to convey the actual eclipse experience. You need a longer view.

On that sunny morning in 1954, there was suddenly a wide, shadowy path across the sky. It ran from the blackened sun, crossed directly above us, and continued on to the west. We could see stars directly overhead; yet on either side of that dark path the sky was still bright blue. The birds stopped singing. All was silent. Even the crowd of spectators on that hill stopped their chatter and stood in total awe. This other-worldly experience lasted just over a minute, and then things slowly returned to normal. But for me, some things were never quite the same again. I've never figured out why, whenever an eclipse happens, TV stations and newspapers don't show that wonderful long view of an eclipse. Maybe they're just overly impressed with the capabilities of their telephoto lenses. Or maybe it's just too hard to capture the subtleties of shadow trails that reach out to you across the sky. Maybe the time of day when the eclipse happens determines whether or not you experience such a spectacular shadow trail.

I think the world today could benefit from getting into the habit of taking a longer view – not just of eclipses, but of history, politics, religion; in fact, of everything. The problem today is certainly not the ability to see things clearly. We can see way too much of celebrities wearing little in the way of clothing. Instead, maybe we need to stand back and look at where our celebrity culture is going. We can watch news clips of dictators behaving badly, but maybe what we really need to do is take a wider view of tyranny and how to deal with it.

Where is this longer view going to come from? Well, it doesn't seem we're likely to get it from the youngsters who dominate the media today. Guess it's up to us seniors. We've got to let people know what we've learned about life. Help them see more of the subtleties and downplay the overly obvious. Our eyesight may not be as good as theirs, but I think vision beats eyesight to kingdom come.

Something to Bring Back from the 40s

Two numbers seem to be skyrocketing these days. Our society can't seem to figure out how to get them under control. I think I've got the answer for both. We just have to bring back an idea from the 1940s. The two numbers I'm referring to are the price of oil and the rate of obesity. If you drive a car or heat with oil, you know all about the first one. If you look around when you're in a crowd, you'll see many examples of the second. The National Center for Health Statistics reported that the average weight for American men ballooned by 25 pounds in the last half century. For American women it grew 24 pounds, and for 10-year-olds 11 pounds.

There seem to be complex international reasons for both of these problems. Oil prices are high because we Americans use a lot of gasoline and therefore have to pay OPEC's prices, competing with countries such as China that have just recently discovered the pleasures of the traffic jam. I blame the rise in obesity on the fact that so many good jobs have gone overseas. Many of us now are able to find employment only in the fast-food business, with the resulting effect on everybody's waistline.

If the baby boomers running our country can't figure out what to do about all this, then it's time for us older people to step forward with the obvious answer. It worked before. Let's bring back rationing. During World War II, things like food and gas and shoes were rationed. (That last one wasn't bad, because it meant that I got to run around barefoot all summer.) Each member of the family received a ration book, with different colored stamps for different items. When my mother sent me to the neighborhood store, the coin purse had to contain not only some cash, but the right number and kind of stamps. Sometimes you got red or blue tokens as "change" for your stamps.

Drivers with "A" stickers on their windshields could buy only four gallons of gas a week. A "B" sticker meant you were an essential war worker, which got you eight gallons. People like doctors, ministers, and (of course) Congressmen could buy even more.

For a while during that time, my dad drove a truck delivering gas to service stations and farms. I remember him sitting at the dining room table at night, pasting hundreds of ration stamps into a big book. Everything had to be accounted for.

Rationing was a bother, but it did help keep prices low and waistlines slim in those days, while also controlling the distribution of essentials that were scarce during the war years. We could do this sort of thing again. If gas were rationed today, we'd be more inclined to walk to where we're going – or at least walk to the nearest bus line. This would save scarce resources and, by reducing demand, lower their price. On top of that, the exercise would do us a world of good.

Distant mega-stores would be supplanted by neighborhood mom and pop groceries like we had in the old days. An extra bonus would be the lift that comes from hearing the owner greet you by name.

If we brought back food rationing today, we wouldn't have to apply it to every kind of food – just anything that comes fried or grilled. Your ration stamps would let you buy, say, one or two or three hamburgers and bags of fries per month (depending on whether they were regular, supersized, or colossal). Soda pop would only be sold in normal-size cups or cans, not in 64-ounce buckets.

These simple steps could solve two of our biggest problems today – our ballooning waistlines and our ballooning dependence on oil. Just imagine what might be accomplished by rationing a few other things as well. For example, I'd like to see a limit on how many "unknown number" telemarketing calls my phone could receive per day, or how many junk mail envelopes could clutter my mailbox.

Yes, those whippersnappers who run things now could do a lot better job if they'd just listen to some of the tried-and-true ideas their elders are willing to share from their past experience.

Taking Family Vacations Down a Generation

When our vacation trips started including our grandchildren in place of our children, things improved quite a bit (please don't mention that to our sons and daughters). Usually, the trouble with grandchildren is this: when you've seen one, you've seen them all. By that I don't mean that they're all alike. Far from it. But you tend to see them at big family occasions – Christmas, weddings, birthdays. So when one grandchild is there, very likely they all are.

Sometimes they squabble a bit, sometimes they play together enthusiastically, but nearly all the time they're very busy. With a houseful of people, you don't really get to know them individually as well as you'd like. This was certainly true in our case, with eleven grandchildren and the majority of them living out of town.

My wife and I came up with a plan a few years ago. We started "borrowing" one grandchild each year to go on vacation with us. It made a world of difference.

The type of vacations we took didn't become anything much different than what we did when our own kids were small. One improvement was that now we did have air conditioning in the car (except for the year when it died on the first day of a 4,800-mile summer trip).

The biggest change was that we traveled with one child instead of six. We no longer spent any energy trying to quell a continuous rolling riot. We could devote ourselves to bonding pleasurably one on one with someone we'd always wanted to know better.

But it wasn't just the difference in numbers that helped. Parents traveling with even just one child are still the authority figures that can inspire conflict.

Grandparents are the fun people who can be talked into things that your parents would never approve. Grandparents can quietly and nonjudgmentally sympathize while you list your grievances with your brother or sister. In the privacy of a car or the silence of a camp, they can focus rapt attention on your dreams for the future.

Now that I think back on it, I have to conclude that parents should only take their kids on vacation if there are no grandparents readily available. Each of our vacation trips with a grandchild came about when they were ten to thirteen years old at the time. That's a wonderful age to get to know somebody. They've outgrown being homesick when away from mom, they're interested in seeing something of the world, and they're not yet too tied down with jobs or dating to get away. They're at an age when they have ideas of their own and are willing to talk about them to a sympathetic ear. What more could you ask of a vacation companion?

Seniors May Find Some New Ways for Getting Citizens Out to Vote

One fall day in 1940, my grandparents got all dressed up and drove their Model A ten miles to town so that one of them could vote for Franklin Delano Roosevelt and the other for Wendell Willkie.

Now, you might think it would have been more sensible to skip voting as long as they were going to cancel each other out. Maybe the incident just showed that even before I came along, my family excelled at failing to communicate with each other. No, I like to think my grandparents knew how their votes would go, but for second-generation Americans like them, the act of voting was in itself simply too important to miss.

Something sure has changed. Nowadays, fewer than half of registered voters bother to turn out for most elections. I think we're poorer for it, as individuals and as a society. But how can those of us who were brought up believing that voting was vital persuade today's crowd to make the effort?

Apparently, the desire to have the best leaders running our city or state or nation isn't important enough to accomplish it. Neither are the contending policies and philosophies of the various parties. Nor is the privilege of exercising a right that few other people in the history of the world have ever had.

If the old-fashioned reasons for voting don't cut it anymore, maybe we need to come up with some new ones more in keeping with whatever motivates people today.

One thing people seem to enjoy doing in the fall is painting their faces and hair strange colors and going to some huge stadium to scream and yell while watching rich guys take their exercise. It shouldn't be too hard to add this approach to elections. You could show your choice by the colors you wear or by standing up in sort of a wave when your candidate's name is called. Results could be displayed instantly on the scoreboard. People might find this way of voting more fun.

To attract young people, voting may have to be tied in with greasy food or loud music. What about drive-through voting booths where the election judge asks your choice over a scratchy-sounding speaker, and then after voting you're rewarded with some fries?

Or maybe people would pay $100 a ticket to get into a big election concert where rich guys break guitars and eardrums while you cast your ballot. Losing candidates get a trip to the mosh pit.

I think my grandchildren might like a computer game version of voting. You start at the lower levels voting for dog catchers and then work your way up to the rooms where you choose municipal judges and city council members, culminating in the exciting corridors of power where you pick the state and national winners. Along the way, you've got to find clues to what the candidates are really talking about and solve mysteries such as what to do with the surplus. Instead of simply voting for your favorite, you could symbolically blast all of the other candidates to smithereens afterwards. (This reflects some actual time-tested customs found in many countries.)

I don't know if any of these settings would have appealed to my grandparents, but I suspect they might help prevent the nearly empty town halls and school gyms we see on election day now.

Increasing the Percentage of Seniors May Be the Cure for Society's ADHD

When our sugary modern diet started causing tooth decay, most towns dealt with it by adding fluoride to their drinking water supply. Well, something in our current lifestyle seems to be causing an epidemic of ADHD – Attention Deficit Hyperactivity Disorder. I wonder if they'll be tempted to start adding Ritalin to our drinking water. I don't think this will be necessary, though, because as the percentage of seniors continues to grow the ADHD problem should get smaller.

You never used to hear about ADHD, but in recent years teachers began reporting that their classrooms were rife with it. However, the epidemic isn't really confined to kids any more. In fact, everybody younger than me seems to be afflicted. People who suffer from

ADHD supposedly show three classic symptoms:

> **They're inattentive** – unable to keep their minds on any one thing for very long.
>
> **They're hyperactive** – always moving or talking.
>
> **They're impulsive** – acting before they think, unable to curb their reactions, hating to wait their turn.

It should be quickly apparent that these three symptoms also happen to be the main features of modern society.

Let's start with inattentive. Everything is geared to a reduced attention span these days. My clock radio used to wake me with a fifteen-minute national newscast. Now, same time same station, it's three minutes.

These guys are no fools. They must have evidence that the audience's attention span is one-fifth as long as it used to be. This also explains the popularity of things like Instant Messaging and fast food.

Secondly, hyperactivity seems to be the rule. It seems like everybody is always on the go these days, driving like maniacs while at the same time talking on the phone. We test our reflexes with video games instead of our intellects with chess. TV commercials make me tired just watching them: everybody rushing around, quick cuts from one scene to another every fraction of a second.

Finally, impulsive reactions are all the rage – including road rage, air rage, and now you even hear about desk rage. Polite behavior and diplomatic discourse apparently take too long to get one's point across.

With these examples in mind, we certainly can't think of ADHD as a problem that only afflicts children. The good news is that when you're about my age you begin to grow immune. For example, it's no longer hard for me to keep my mind on one thing at a time. One at a time is about my limit, in fact. Say I'm reading an interesting article in the paper. I'm not bothered by intrusive thoughts reminding me that I'm supposed to be doing some chore or other right now.

Hyperactivity is another fault I'm able to avoid. I've developed the discipline to sit for long periods in front of the TV without moving a muscle except in my right thumb.

Impulsive actions – in fact actions of any kind – are seldom a problem. If someone jumps in front of me in line at the store, it just gives me another minute to pause and try to remember what I came there for.

Maybe my generation holds the cure for ADHD. Which would you rather use – Ritalin added to your drinking water, or your already-implanted gene for codgerhood?

Seniors May Hold the Answers to the World's Energy Crisis

One of the many crises facing the world these days is a shortage of energy. My generation could undoubtedly provide some ideas on how to solve this little problem, since most of us routinely have to deal with a shortage of energy. The principles are about the same, whether we're talking human bodies or electric power. The tricks that help older folks get through their personal energy crises should work for everyone else too. Let's review a few of them.

1. Just say no.
This phrase, made famous in the 1980's by Nancy Reagan to promote the war on drugs, has proved inspiring to us seniors in many

other ways as well. When your peers pressure you to take a grueling hike through a park or mall, or they try to get you to experiment with tennis and aerobics, it can take real courage to resist. But we do it, because we learned long ago from the nation's First Lady the importance of knowing how to "just say no." The energy we save by eliminating all that exercise can be used instead to turn pages of a book or flip channels on a TV remote.

2. Quit working.
Retirement is an obvious way to burn far less energy. Most of my friends have mastered this. If more people retired, whole buildings downtown could close down and there would be a lot less traffic on the streets. Think how much less energy would be needed.

3. Migrate with the birds.
When members of my generation find that it takes too much energy to shovel snow or pile on layers of clothing, many of us mimic the birds and migrate to warmer climes until things warm up and settle down again back home.

4. Sleep with the birds.
Older people are notorious for conserving their energy by turning in early. Restaurants recognize this by having their "senior special" prices good at around 4:00 or 5:00 p.m. If everybody followed the example of seniors, cities would only need enough electricity to keep things humming until the six o'clock news is over.

5. Senior living.
If all else fails, everyone could learn how to cluster in tiny apartments, taking most of their meals and entertainment together. Bingo requires practically no electrical power – especially if you play it early enough in the day (see tip number 4). If society wants to nip an energy crisis in the bud, what makes more sense than to follow the example of people who

are old enough to have learned how to exert as little energy as possible?

What Seniors Have to Teach Bulls, Reunions, and Olympians

Two bulls were standing on a hill. Down below, they saw a green pasture with a herd of cows. The young bull pawed the ground in excitement. *"I'm going to gallop down there and do one of those cows!"* he snorted.

The old bull replied, *"Silly boy. Why don't we WALK down there and do ALL of them?"*

Age has always contributed a knack for grasping how to get the most out of a situation by concentrating on the essentials. If the young would only listen, they could have more fun with a lot less effort.

Another example (although unfortunately far less sexy) that occurs to me is the class reunion. My high school classmates used to get together every five years in the typical fancy reunion. It took us fifty years to figure out what was really fun about reunions and what was not. Now, we've got it down pat.

Our reunions used to be held at some fancy restaurant or clubhouse. Weeks beforehand, there were questionnaires to fill out so that a booklet could be printed and handed out at the dinner. You could brag about your successful career, your brilliant kids, your fascinating travels. At the reunion, you dressed to the nines and danced to the music of a live band. It was a great celebration. But exactly what were we celebrating? Putting on the dog or renewing old friendships?

As years went by, many classmates began to be frustrated with the way things were done. What we really wanted to do was sit and chat, which was hard to do over the noise of a band. As we approached codgerhood, even getting all dressed up was a chore, and a fancy meal might or might not fit with what our doctor said we could eat. And not much was happening in our lives that we needed to brag about in that reunion booklet. Saddest of all was the realization that some of our number might not be here to visit with five years from now, so a yearly chat was better.

After our fifty-year reunion we decided to stick with the best parts of reunions and leave out the irritating parts. It's great! What we've left out are things like the questionnaires to fill out, the noisy music, the expensive dinner. We concentrate on the positive bits like chatting with old friends and renewing youthful memories. We simply get together at the home of one of our classmates or at an inexpensive restaurant. Everybody brings something for the pot-luck dinner. And the best part is that we get together every year instead of every five. Hey, as the old bull explained, if it's fun and you find a way to make it easier, why not do it more often? I think this lesson that took our classmates fifty years to learn ought to be shared with the rest of the world, if it will listen.

Take the Olympics. What are they really about? Athletic performance on the track, in the pool, on the field. Everything else is extraneous. The Olympics don't need to be hosted in expensive new stadiums, and cities shouldn't have to go through a lot of rebuilding and beautification or stage elaborate parades. None of that stuff has anything to do with athletics.

Athletes could do their running, swimming, or jumping in their own home towns. Then they could phone their times in to some central place where the Olympic people could tabulate all the records. Team sports might be a little more complicated to handle that way, but I'm pretty sure it would be simpler and cheaper to have one team visit another team's city to compete than to have every team in the world meet at the same place.

I can picture how much fun it would be to go to some venue at my home town each year to watch our local athletes competing against the world. In place of elaborate opening and closing ceremonies, we'd just have a mass pot luck dinner where everybody brought a hot dish. (That's Minnesotan for casserole. Non-Minnesotans could celebrate in their own local culinary style.)

For many years, the Olympic motto of "Faster, higher, stronger" has inspired the youth of the world. But it may be time for a new motto: "Simpler, cheaper, easier." To achieve that, just ask the people who've had to learn those skills. In other words, ask somebody older.

Forgetfulness Is Vital

Seniors have so much to contribute to the world, if only people would pay attention. I'm not talking about whatever stack of wisdom and experience we've accumulated, although that could just possibly be worth something. I'm talking about specific abilities and talents we have that younger people lack.

I know, most people assume that natural abilities tend to decrease, not increase, when you get older. That just shows how misunderstood we seniors are. There are lots of important things that we do better than anyone else. A prime example is the ability to forget. I'm not kidding – this is an important function that just may turn out to be a key to the future of society.

I'm worried that younger people nowadays have way too much to remember. It's hard for them to avoid it, exposed as they are to constant stimuli. It's important to remember the good advice that Sherlock Holmes gave Dr. Watson in Arthur Conan Doyle's first story, "A Study in Scarlet."

"You see," said Holmes, *"I consider that a man's brain originally is like a little empty attic, and you have to stock it with such furniture as you choose. A fool takes in all the lumber of every sort that he comes across, so that the knowledge which might be useful to him gets crowded out... Now the skillful workman is very careful indeed as to what he takes into his brain-attic."* Holmes went on to explain: *"It is a mistake to think that this little room has elastic walls and can distend to any extent... It is of the highest importance, therefore, not to have useless facts elbowing out the useful ones."*

For most of the younger generation, it's too late to follow Sherlock's advice to simply avoid filling up their brains with excessive stuff. TV, comics, and even textbooks have already done their insidious work. Those mental attics are overflowing. Young people need to free up more room in their attics by forgetting some things. And that just happens to be a skill that seniors are really good at. I'm not sure just how we could impart our forgetfulness to younger folks. Transferring an ability – whether it's painting watercolors, composing symphonies, or forgetting things you read or hear – is much more complicated than just teaching some facts.

I'm thinking of putting together a team of seniors who are expert in different types of forgetting. My own specialty is woolgathering. This technique involves daydreaming about some comfortable subject until you forget whatever it was that was trying to hold your attention. Other experts on our team might specialize in the forgetting of superfluous phone numbers, bills to pay that cause concern, or incidents that are embarrassing. Through demonstrations, we could perhaps teach a class of younger people how to empty their mental attics of superfluous facts. I'm sure Sherlock Holmes would approve.

But teaching the general population how to forget some things could actually accomplish a lot more than simply leaving room in their minds for more important knowledge. It could lead to the realization of what every beauty-contest contestant says is her dream – peace in the world.

Most human conflicts could be avoided if people were able to forget about disputes or insults that irritated them. Wars have mostly been caused by personal disputes between rulers. The world's awful religious conflicts – Shiite versus Sunni in Iraq, or before that Anglican versus Catholic in Ireland, or before that the Hundred Years War in Europe – often originated not so much through tremendously profound differences in doctrine, but through personal disagreements between individuals.

All those terrible conflicts could have ended quickly if the people involved in the original spats had been able to forget whatever it was that made them angry. They would never have passed their irritation on to their successors for ages afterward. That's why learning to forget is so profoundly important. We seniors need to share our very special ability with the world. I'm going to get a bunch of my friends together and start working on our anti-memory seminar. Now, where do you suppose I put their phone numbers?

Needed: A Group for Grumps

The hottest thing these days on the Internet – or just about anywhere else – is social networking.

Millions of people spend hours chatting on their Facebook walls, posting brief tweets on Twitter, or contacting their group on Instagram. People in business keep in touch through sites like LinkedIn and Facebook. In fact, the online reference book Wikipedia lists hundreds of social networking sites. And that's all good. I haven't been able to find the time to really get involved myself, but my wife totally enjoys these sites. She has daily contact with many friends and relatives through Facebook, and with high school acquaintances on Classmates. Some of these are people she hasn't seen in years, but now it's like they're next-door neighbors.

I enjoy her networking vicariously. And in my own brief forays online, I enjoy watching how people greet their friends each morning, chatter periodically during the day, and bid each other good night at bedtime. They have developed close relationships with folks they would never even have known otherwise.

In spite of all this, I think there's something wrong. A major segment of society is being left out. How come there are 150 social networking groups, and apparently not a single anti-social networking group? Does that seem fair? Cranky people have needs and rights too. Even if someone's not perfect, attention must be paid (as Willy Loman's wife Linda proclaimed in "Death of a Salesman").

I think it's high time somebody started a forum for anti-social networking. First off, it seems the right thing to do in order to reduce that 150-to-zero imbalance between social and anti-social groups. Besides, filling a huge unmet need like this could possibly end up being very lucrative.

The anti-social network could be sort of like Facebook (maybe we could call it the "In-Your-Face Book"). The difference would be that the writing you put on someone's wall would be more like what you see scrawled on walls along the freeway.

Or our network could be sort of like Twitter. We could call it "Twerp." Crotchety people wouldn't have a problem at all with limiting their note to a certain number of characters. Most would just say something like "Yada-yada-yada" or "Humph."

I know quite a few people who would probably be naturals for this type of network. At least their style of communication would be right. Getting them to join our group – or any group for that matter – might be more of a challenge.

Grown-Ups Can Teach Youngsters More by What They Do Than by What They Say

If you're ever trying to convey a lesson to your kids, grandkids, or a group you belong to, the important thing to understand is that you'll probably teach more by what you do than by anything you say.

This truth was brought home to me way back in 1952, at my high school graduation ceremony. The guest speaker did his best to enlighten and inspire us. He was a college president, witty and sophisticated. He didn't really talk directly to us graduates sitting solemnly behind him on the stage, but stood facing our parents out in the audience. I don't remember a thing he said, but I'll never forget the message his body language delivered as he stood there behind the lectern.

As he spoke, those of us sitting behind him could see his legs twisting ever more tightly into a corkscrew configuration. While his words sparkled and his tone was smooth and relaxed, his contortions revealed he was either very nervous or he really, really had to go. From this we learned that, no matter what kind of stress or pain you're under, it's possible to carry on and show a brave front to the world. We also learned the corollary of that: no matter how great you look to the world, there are always people who can see the ridiculous side of you. Maybe that's as profound a lesson as you can expect to get from any commencement speaker.

Part Three:
Ways to Help Make the Journey Fun

There are a few things you can try
when starting that long downhill run,
that pretty soon will show you why
this part of life is filled with fun

Don't Rest, Relax!

We spend a weekend occasionally visiting our daughter and her family at a cabin they own near Prairie Du Chien, Wisconsin. It's right on the Mississippi River, and the scenery is extraordinarily beautiful. Everybody loves the place, and considers it a wonderful getaway from the world. And yet, it's not what you would normally consider peaceful.

In front of the cabin, towboats chug up and down the river pushing long lines of barges. Speedboats and jet skis race by. Neighbors are constantly launching or retrieving their watercraft at a nearby ramp. A block away, fast trains whistle every few minutes on one of the busiest rail lines in the country.

On top of this, when my daughter and her husband spend time at their cabin, they usually are surrounded by multitudes of family and friends who somehow need to be fed and entertained. In spite of all this apparent stress and turmoil, they find their time at the cabin happy and soothing. How can this be?

I learned the answer to that many years ago while still working in the corporate world. Back in the 1970s and '80s, my team and I produced audio visuals for a large insurance company. Once or twice a year, we went out of town to stage a convention for our agents. In those days, multi-image slide shows were all the rage. We had a massive rear-projection screen the width of a stage. Behind it were 16 to 20 slide projectors and a movie projector, plus our sound system and a primitive computer that controlled it all.

A typical day's program on stage included some very elaborate slide shows – thematics, sales-leader recognition pieces, and promotions for the next year's conference site. Usually these had been produced and programmed beforehand. However, it wasn't until we were on site that we could combine the programs for all these shows, plus the live cues for background images between shows as well as speaker support slides, together into one massive program. Then we had to plan our slide-tray changes and rehearse it all. This involved grueling hours of work. After one all-night programming session followed by a long day of staging the event, I was more than ready to turn in early to catch up on some sleep. The next morning, I found out to my amazement that John, one of my staff, had partied all night at cocktail soirees hosted by the company's various agencies.

"How could you possibly stay up two whole nights in a row?" I asked him.

"Well, you see," he explained with a smile, *"there's rest and there's relaxation. I decided that what I needed was relaxation."*

And I believe that explains why a vacation getaway is enjoyable even when it's full of hectic activity. It may not be any more restful than work, but it's definitely more relaxing. You're there because you want to be, and your intent is to have fun. At work, you're doing what you have to, not what you choose to. That makes all the difference. The same thing applies to retirement. My wife and I definitely do not have a restful retirement. We're as busy as ever. Visiting family. Partying with friends. Gardening. Traveling. Working with civic and church groups. There still are tasks and deadlines, like when we had regular jobs. But these are OUR tasks and deadlines. Being busy may not be as restful as sitting in a recliner, but like my friend John, we've learned that sometimes there are things more rewarding than rest.

Retirement is a blessing somewhat like getting away to that vacation hideaway on the river. It's wonderful, not because you get to do nothing, but because you get to CHOOSE what you want to do. It's peaceful not because there's no noise, but because you learn to enjoy the noise you hear. We could all learn a lesson from John. In all stages of life, there's rest and there's relaxation. Relaxation is more fun.

Marriage Is like Food

Now, I suppose you're thinking that when I say *"marriage is like food"* I mean that marriage is nourishing, it sustains us, and when it's done well it makes life infinitely more interesting and pleasurable. Well, of course all of that is true. But what I really had in mind was a little more prosaic. I was thinking that marriage has a lot in common with that can of beans on your pantry shelf.

Before the reader takes offense (especially if the reader is someone I'm married to), let me explain. First, I have to give you a little history that I ran across in Discover Magazine several years ago.

Back in 1810, Peter Durand from Britain patented his great new invention: the tin can. Don't laugh, it was a pretty big deal. Food could now be sealed up and safely preserved for a long time, and it could be done quickly and in great quantities. It was a wonderful idea. Unfortunately, it wasn't until 1858 that Ezra Warner from Connecticut patented the can opener.

Just think – for almost five decades, there was all this wonderfully preserved food but no convenient way to get at it. How did people open cans during those years? Hack them with axes? Pound them with rocks? Or did they just save them on the groaning shelves of their cupboards in the hope that someday there would be a way to open them? It's amazing that a wonderful thing like the tin can didn't really become fully practical and easy to use until almost fifty years after it was invented.

Well, since my wife and I have been married for well over half a century, it occurs to me that marriage, like the tin can, gets much more workable after that amount of time. This is true on many different levels. Take communications. Newlyweds struggle mightily – and often in vain – to figure out what their spouses are really saying. Often the problem is that they're not really saying anything, but should be.

For example, when Mickey and I got married, she was used to cooking for four people. Her mother worked, so when Mickey got home from her high school or college classes, she started dinner for her parents, herself, and her brother. After our wedding, she still tended to cook about the right amount for four people.

Now, I had been brought up as a member of the "clean plate club," which was promoted during World War II to keep kids from wasting food. So I manfully ate the big dinner she cooked every night. Then, since I ate all the food in sight, she thought she'd better fix a little more the next time. This went on for a few months, while I gained at least forty pounds. Somehow, we finally talked about the situation and ended the cycle of caloric escalation.

After fifty years or more, a wife no longer makes the mistake of failing to discuss any of her husband's behavior about which she has any doubts or misgivings. But communication in marriage doesn't improve only because you're more likely to be open about things you didn't talk about before. You also get a lot more efficient at the whole process. After fifty years or so, a wife can convey paragraphs in a glance, volumes in a facial expression. Even husbands can sometimes be surprisingly articulate with a grunt or shrug.

Marriage gets more efficient and workable in other ways, too. Fighting, for example. Every couple occasionally has a dispute about something or other. Fights early in a marriage are devastating and emotional. It takes a week to get over a minor scrap. After fifty years, you can have a relatively knock-down-and-drag-out battle some morning, and by lunch time you can't remember what it was about. In other words, once you get really good at a relationship, you can handle all phases of it in less time. And I do mean "all phases."

Let's see, what aspects of married life haven't we touched on yet? Oh yes, that! I'll wait now while all readers under the age of fifty leave the room. Tum, de dum, de dum... Are they gone? Okay, we can continue.

The reason we can't talk to those relative youngsters about having a love life after five decades or more of marriage is that all grown children devoutly believe that nothing of that sort ever happens in their parents' bedroom.

The fact is that this aspect of marriage, like all the others, tends to remain pleasurable while getting even more efficient over the years. So, what's wrong if "efficient" might mean it could go a little quicker? Isn't that the definition of efficiency?

Anyhow, I'm sure these few examples have shown you the lesson that all married people should take from the lowly tin can. What starts out as a beautiful idea really needs to stick around for a few years to reach its potential. Somehow I don't think frozen TV dinners will ever convey as important a lesson.

The Strangest Little Things Can Take You Back in Time

While visiting our youngest son and his wife one Thanksgiving, I think we caught a glimpse of the fountain of youth. It was located at the State Fair Grounds near their home. Not everybody was affected equally. We guys who were there found ourselves transported back to about the ninth grade. The gals, who always seem to know more about keeping or regaining their youth, went back to an even younger age.

The event that set off this time travel was the biggest craft fair I've ever seen. A dozen large buildings and tents were packed with the booths of crafters from all over the country. Thousands of people poured through the offerings seeking the perfect Christmas present or decorative doodad.

It was my daughter-in-law who pointed out to us the clusters of men standing at the ends of the aisles in each of the buildings. To me, they looked just like the stag line on the fringe of the dance floor at a ninth grade party.

Some stared into space with expressions that told of places they'd rather be. Others chatted with each other while drinking soda pop. Still others studied the lively action on the floor as though they wished they had the courage to join in.

I'm proud to say that my son and I did not stand with the wallflowers. Like the braver souls at those ninth grade parties, we did our best to shuffle along in step with our partners without necessarily understanding what was going on.

While the men attending the show seemed temporarily returned to the ninth grade, the women found themselves somewhere back in the halcyon days of elementary school. They joyously flitted about admiring all sorts of dolls and figurines. Santas were everywhere, along with quaint old-fashioned games, toys, and dollhouses. There were enough cute decorative gimcracks to fill a thousand little girls' bedrooms. Exploring this wondrous toyland put a spring in their steps and peals of excitement in their voices.

I'd have to say that the girls came out better on this one than us. Early childhood is a great time of life to relive. Ninth grade is one of the worst. But that doesn't mean we guys always lose out on this kind of thing.

When you think about it, all of us run into opportunities to revisit our youth every day. Maybe a baseball game takes you back to the first one you attended with your mom and dad. A picnic brings memories of vacations in the old family car. Watching your

Downhill Is Where the Fun Is

grandkids splash at a water park reminds you of what it was like at the old swimming hole in the days before you worried about getting too much sun.

We're actually pretty lucky. There are only a few things that can make us old. Hardening of the attitudes. Softening of the enthusiasm. Shrinkage of the curiosity. But there's almost no end of things that can make us young again if we let them.

Are You a "Take Care" or a "Bye-Bye" Person?

Everybody knows that during a conversation we can show people how we feel about something. Not everyone realizes that, through a couple of words that we say without thinking when we sign off from a conversation, we can reveal even more about ourselves.

For example, my wife and I recently got an e-mail from an old friend and former neighbor. She ended it, "Take care…" Those two words expressed her personality to a T. As a nurse, she was always involved in taking care of others. As a rather starchy Scandinavian, she was always controlled, helpful, judicious, and more than willing to give advice. She's very much a "Take care" sort of person.

Years ago, I worked for the Midwestern regional office of a big corporation that had its headquarters in New Jersey. All the people from the corporate headquarters ended their phone conversations with "Take care."

I don't think they meant it in quite the same way as our nurse friend. With them, it was more of a "Watch your step, don't trust anyone, I'm telling you this for your own good because I know more than you do" kind of thing.

Most of my colleagues in the regional office played right into the corporate people's hands by ending with "Bye bye!" They seemed to be saying, "Yes, you are superior and I'm a childlike but friendly hick, so be gentle with me."

When people transferred from the regional office to corporate headquarters, you could tell they were assimilated when they changed from *"Bye bye!"* to *"Take care."* I always looked on it as a loss of innocence. Corporate people who transferred to the Midwest usually stayed "Take care" people. Loss of cynicism takes longer than loss of innocence, I guess. All of this led me to examine how I ended my own conversations. It turned out I usually said "So long." This may have been a subconscious recognition that I had been working there for too many years. I'm pretty certain it wasn't due to any Freudian boastfulness.

Now that I'm retired from the corporate world while still working on things I like to do, I find myself signing off most conversations with *"Take it easy."* I suppose this expresses the hope that the other person can arrive at the relaxed, yet busy, life style that I enjoy.

When I talk to my wife, it's a slightly different story. Whenever we part, she says *"Be good,"* which recognizes my tendency toward misbehavior and her own responsibility for keeping it in check. I reply, *"Have fun!"* This is probably my way of saying that a little misbehavior isn't really so bad, is it? Please?

A lot of people now end conversations with *"Have a nice day."* I think it combines the "Bye bye" person's naive friendliness with the "Take care" person's need to give advice. It suggests someone on the border between child and adult. I wonder if, over the years, they tend to change to "Make sure you have a nice day," then "Take care to have a nice day," and finally end up with just "Take care."

Try listening to how you end your conversations. You never know what you might find out about yourself. Have fun!

Be Sensible and Grow Old or Be Silly and Stay Young

As I look around at the people I've known for many years, it's the sensible ones who seem to be getting old. The ones who don't know any better are forcing themselves to stay young. That's because they keep on doing the things they don't need to do any more. The things that cause pain and inconvenience. The things that put them at risk. The things that disrupt the order of their lives.

For example, a sensible body stops exercising when its joints and muscles no longer enjoy the process. Why make tired legs run when nothing is chasing you, or arthritic arms lift things when there's no pay involved? Why chew broccoli when there's no longer your mom around to force you? It's silly to make your body do such unpleasant things.

By the same token, a sensible mind realizes when it has earned the right to relax and be comfortable with what it already knows. An unstable one keeps poking around at new ideas even when they challenge favorite beliefs.

A sensible spirit is cautious about love, because it has learned a lesson from all those times when it has been disillusioned. A naive spirit carelessly gives love to a person, group, or cause without worrying enough about the consequences.

When you put them all together – body, mind, and spirit – in a sensible way, you have a person who knows how to relax and accept old age. A rash person keeps stirring the pot. With all that activity, he or she will probably never be able to fully retire or even get old.

Groups of people can act young or old, too. Put together a bunch of sensible relatives, and you have a family that respects each other's space. They like each other, but maintain a healthy distance. Some overly enthusiastic families don't seem to keep any distance at all. They're always doing things together. They even get sentimental over each other's irritating little foibles.

Put together enough sensible families, and you have a sensible society. Rule of law and all that. A rash young society goes out on a limb by offering freedom to people who don't really deserve it, encouraging responsibility on the part of those who don't much want to exercise it, and providing for the needy even when it becomes way too expensive.

Whether you're talking about a body, mind, or spirit, a person, family, or society, the mature attitude is to quit struggling when the cost becomes too great. We're not suddenly unable to walk to the store or play ball with the kids or fall in love or volunteer at the food shelf. It's just that there comes a time when it's painful or bothersome to do these things. So you stop doing them, and then you forget how.

The immature attitude doesn't see that the cost is too great. When life makes you tired or hurt, you just keep going. Whatever you want to do may not be as easy or as fast or as beautiful as before, but it's important to do it anyway. The only trouble is, forcing yourself to do all that extra living may mean that your new recliner is in danger of going to waste.

Some days I see the wisdom of the sensible approach. Some days I embrace the beauty of the immature approach. But I'm pretty sure that my immature friends are having more fun than the sensible ones.

Cruising Through Retirement

Does the thought of having to move into an assisted living apartment or nursing home have you scared silly? If and when that day does come (hopefully way off in the future), it may not be as bad as you expect.

Want to see a preview of what it'll be like? Simply take a cruise. Those long white ships are like time machines that can transport you into the future. It works for people in any age group, and it works with both ocean and river cruises.

One young couple we met on an ocean cruise told us, *"We hardly ever see our children since we came on board. The kids are kept busy with so many wonderful activities and parties, often until late at night."* This couple didn't realize it, but they had just been transported ahead to their middle-aged days when their family will be grown up and busy with their own lives.

Middle-aged passengers who were taking a vacation from their demanding careers got a feel for what it will be like to retire. In effect, the folks who run the ship told them the same thing that their employers will someday: *"It's time for you to just sit back and relax. We have young people from many different countries who will take care of all the work that needs to be done."*

Those of us who are already retired also got a strong glimpse of our future. To make sure we don't miss this lesson, every cruise ship passageway has the same kind of support bars along the walls that you find in the hallways of nursing homes. In addition, cruise directors and activity leaders display the same exaggerated air of enthusiasm that is found among the staff of nursing homes. They must have studied at the same schools, or maybe they take the same kind of pills.

Cruise ships always seem to stage at least as many bingo games per day as nursing homes do. Cruise ships feature a mind-numbing array of excursions, activities, and entertainments, just as good nursing homes do. Nursing homes (at least the one my dad was in during his final months) offer a number of opportunities each day for snacking and coffee breaks in addition to the regular three meals. Cruise ships, of course, are notorious for their endless supply of food.

Cruise ship cabins also give you a chance to live in a lot less space than you're used to, which should help you make the transition to a nursing home.

All of this is good preparation for seeing how well you will be able to adjust to the later stages of your life.

If you want to look even further ahead, a river cruise can provide the confusion that comes from waking each day in a totally new city with unfamiliar landmarks. Do you see it as frightening, or as a perpetually new set of wonders to discover? Get used to looking at daily confusion in a positive way now, before you really have to.

When my dad was in the nursing home, he wasn't particularly happy with his life. I think this was because he didn't really like to be around outgoing, enthusiastic people or a lot of activity. He should have gone on some cruises years before to help prepare himself.

My wife and I won't fall into that trap. We hope to take frequent refresher courses in how to cruise happily through our later years.

In my younger days, vacations nearly always involved camping trips with our six kids. Even after Mickey and I were back on our own, we never went on trips organized and led by a tour group. I insisted that we make our travel arrangements ourselves as we went along. Even on our sorties overseas, we figured out rail schedules or driving routes on our own. The thought of following some bossy martinet around based on his schedule *("All rrright! Everybody into ze bus!")* was out of the question.

Even MORE out of the question would have been joining a tour group that caters to seniors. Most of the friends we've hung around with as adults have tended to be a decade or two younger than us. I imagined that a senior tour group would resemble a bunch of shuffling zombies. Then one year we took a river cruise on the Danube with a senior group and I found out I'd never been more wrong. First of all, it's kind of nice to be spoiled by tour directors who pick you up at the airport, see that your luggage goes to the right cabin on your boat, and watch over every aspect of your trip to see that nothing goes awry.

Next, the type of seniors who take this kind of tour are the most young-at-heart, enthusiastic and fun-loving bunch of people you're ever likely to meet. Most had been on many trips with this same tour company, and obviously knew how to enjoy it to the hilt.

People-Seeing Beats Sightseeing!

On all our previous trips, we concentrated on sightseeing. We were pretty successful at that, but we didn't really get to know many of the local folks very well. This trip not only offered plenty of sightseeing, but the people we met were an unexpected and wonderful benefit.

Our tour directors were fountains of information and came from the areas we visited (Hungary, Croatia, Serbia, Bulgaria, and Romania). At every port, our busses had local guides who not only pointed out the monuments and scenery but filled us in on the local culture, customs, politics, personalities, and history. There were college students who came on board the ship to tell us about their lives after the transition from communism to democracy. We broke into small groups and had lunch with Croation families in their homes. We stopped at many places where we were entertained by local dancers, singers, and musicians. And when we weren't being entertained and taught by these local people, we spent time with a boatload of fascinating Americans who have seen just about every part of the world. After this trip, meeting people became much more important to us than seeing the sights.

Growth Calls for Change

Looking back, I don't really know why it took me so long to accept the idea of this new (for me) kind of vacation. I've always believed in the need for change.

In fact, that was the reason for my retiring from a secure corporate job back when I was 55. It wasn't a bad job, but I had been sitting there at the same level for the previous ten years. After a good deal of thought, I came up with the Adams Law of Corporate Motion: If you notice that you haven't changed your position in the last ten years, you ought to consider the possibility that you're dead. I didn't like the implications of that, so I left the corporate world and struck out on my own. It's been a lot more fun.

Now, I think it's time to formulate the Adams Law of Vacations: If your last ten vacations have been very similar to each other, maybe what you've really been doing is just trudging off to work in a different way.

Act Your Age – or Not

When I was a kid, my mother often told me *"Act your age."* I soon figured out that she didn't really mean that I should act my chronological age. I was already doing that, which was what led to the trouble in the first place. I think she really wanted me to act like some more dignified age – probably about thirty.

Now that I'm approaching the other end of the age continuum, it seems that similar rules apply. It's not proper to behave in a way that reflects your actual number of years. But this time, you're supposed to act younger instead of older.

Acting "old" has come to mean being cranky, narrow minded, and set in your ways. I recently heard a twenty-something guy described as an "old man" just because there are very few kinds of food he is willing to eat.

Being something of an old man myself, I don't exactly appreciate that my group has become the symbol for undesirable traits. You no longer hear very many jokes about stingy Scots, drunken Irish, dumb Poles, and so on. Thank goodness, people have drifted away from that sort of stereotype. Unfortunately, elders are apparently still fair game.

One solution is for us not to act our current age in public. It should actually be easy for us to pull it off. We know how to act every age, since we've already experienced nearly all of them. At any moment, we can choose whether to act with the enthusiasm of a teen, the ambition of a young adult, or the dignity of a middle-ager. We've been through all that and should be expert at it.

But still, we should occasionally be entitled to act our own age, and do it with pride. Of course, we may have to do it at a time and place when no other age groups can see us.

A while ago, I had a chance to do just that. My wife and I drove to Arizona to visit with a group of people with whom we had gone to high school in Minnesota. Although the others at the gathering have all become seasonal or permanent refugees from the cold, we still had a great deal in common with them. And one of the neat features of this reunion was that, in the privacy of our group, we could act any age we chose without anyone criticizing us.

We started out acting our current age while sitting on the patio talking. Yes, there was a certain amount of complaining about physical infirmities, grousing about the state of society today, and praising the good old days. And it was all okay. We could cut loose and act our age with no youngsters there to hear and poke fun at us.

Later, to show our versatility, we enjoyed reliving some of the other ages we've gone through. We had a big pot-luck dinner just like middle-aged people habitually do, and then plunged into lavish amounts of cake and ice cream like a bunch of kids. It was great.

I think this is exactly what all older people need to do: Get together with our peers. Act our age all we want, with nobody younger around to see and hear. Then, to ease our way back to the way we must act in front of the world, we can conclude the session by moving backward in time through some of our younger stages.

Maybe we should start having secret senior meetings in every town. People will wonder what rituals go on during our ceremonies. We'll never tell them that we're doing something forbidden – acting our age.

Can the Internet Provide a New Motto for Our Time?

When my generation was starting out, we were advised to look in the mirror and say, *"Every day, in every way, I'm getting better and better.*" It's a beautiful thought, but somehow it wasn't entirely convincing even then. Now that the years and gravity have left their mark, it's even harder to say it with a straight face. I wonder if we need a new mantra, maybe something a little more practical.

It's just possible that the Internet may have provided it. The technical wizard who set up my Web site years ago explained it to me. It seems that when you design a page for the Internet, you have to take into account the fact that not everybody will be looking at that page with the latest equipment and software. The goal is to make that page still look pretty good even to somebody who is using an old version of a browser, a slow computer, and a less-than-sharp monitor.

If your work still looks okay under those conditions, it's said to be capable of "degrading gracefully." That phrase struck me as very powerful. Why can't it apply to people as well as Web pages? "Every day, in every way, I'm degrading very gracefully." It's not as lofty as "getting better and better," but it's definitely more attainable.

"Getting better and better" would imply that my hair is growing back. "Degrading gracefully" simply requires that I manage to look somewhat okay without it. "Getting better and better" makes me think that someday I should be running marathons. "Degrading gracefully" only means I should be able to move around without displaying too much of a codger shuffle.

"Getting better and better in every way" commits me to becoming a Renaissance person able to paint a portrait while solving binomial equations in my head. "Degrading gracefully" can be achieved if I pick up after myself and usually remember what day it is.

Maybe it's not just my generation that ought to switch mottos, but the whole human race. For example, we could face up to the fact that we're not exactly making the environment better and better. Perhaps it's time to settle for a little graceful degradation and learn to accept global warming and a smidgeon of arsenic in the water. It might also be time to admit that we've lost the war on poverty that we declared long ago. But our homeless people can perhaps take solace in the fact that we're working at having a lighter tax burden. That's somewhat graceful, isn't it?

We haven't succeeded in stamping out war and disease. But where once we were horrified by the Bubonic Plague and the Holocaust, we now are developing the ability to take AIDS and ethnic cleansing in stride. That's surely grace in the face of degradation.

So, what do you think? Should we give up on the impossible dream of getting better and better every day in every way? Would it be better to reach our goals by lowering them, and aim for degrading gracefully?

Hmmmm. Nah, I guess not.

How Do We Preserve the Human Race? Eating More Dessert.

For a long time now, my wife has been trying to convince me that I'm putting on weight. She actually had me believing it's my own fault that I have more trouble getting into airline or theater seats than I did years ago.

Now I know the truth. It's not that I'm getting bigger. The rest of the world is getting smaller. I'll bet the part of me that tries to fit into those cramped seats hasn't changed at all. The seats, like everything else nowadays, are smaller than before. An example of how the world is getting smaller could be seen in a paper published a few years ago by two nutrition experts from Johns Hopkins. After studying data from the Miss America Pageant over the years, they concluded that Miss America winners are getting skinnier. In fact, many are downright undernourished.

The researchers calculated the body mass index (BMI) of all the Miss Americas. It turns out that back in the 1920s, contestants had BMIs in the normal range, which is 20 to 25. But in more recent years, many were below 18.5, which is considered undernourished. It's not just the Miss Americas who are getting smaller. Look at all the new up-and-coming stars in the entertainment world. They seem to be getting skinnier all the time, at least from the viewpoint of people like me.

Business is getting smaller too. Over the last decade or two, big companies laid off workers by the thousands. It was the little home-based businesses that became the fastest-growing part of the economy. We're heading back to the pre-industrial days of cottage enterprises. After AT&T gets rid of its last employee, we'll all be selling phone cards to each other from our homes.

They say that in the twilight of the giant dinosaurs, a little rat-like creature scurried unnoticed under their feet — the first mammals. The descendants of these mammals grew larger and smarter and eventually took over the world. Meanwhile, the dinosaurs began diminishing until they evolved into today's chickens and chickadees.

Well, now we've had our turn at the top. Maybe it's humanity's time to shrink down to insignificance and give some other species our place. Those science-fiction movies about people cowering from giant cockroaches or spiders may just be a glimpse of the future.

Luckily, there are a few of us able to see what's happening in time to warn the rest. Like the Johns Hopkins scientists who blew the whistle on Miss America. Or people like me who notice that airline seats are shrinking in size. The rest of you must decide to fight this whole shrinking trend before it's too late. With your calorie-counting charts and points-calculating slide rules and fat-absorbing pills, you're playing right into the hands of those little insects that are just waiting to take over the world.

When Miss America displays the curves of a Rubens or Rembrandt model, when people shaped like Winston Churchill or William Howard Taft take over politics again, I'll know that my crusade to save the human race is having some effect. Maybe then I'll even be able to talk my wife into letting me have dessert more often.

Sometimes Striking out Beats Drawing a Walk

Now that I'm in my mid-80s, I find that a lot of people are advising me to take it easy. My kind family members insist on doing many of the chores around our house, my doting wife does all our driving, and the company that once employed me arranged for me to receive a small pension check each month without my showing up for work at all. But somehow I don't feel comfortable with the idea of living a completely passive life. I think it's important to find ways to be active.

This whole subject sort of reminds me of an incident I saw years ago at our granddaughter's slow-pitch softball game. One of the parents did a rather disturbing thing. No, he didn't get into a fight with another parent. He didn't threaten the umpire. He didn't even holler at his daughter to be more aggressive, as several other parents did. No, what he did was just the opposite. He kept telling her to be more passive.

"Don't swing at the ball!" he would shout when she was at the plate. "NEVER swing at the ball." In a way, he had a point. These were elementary-school players. Although our granddaughter was, of course, a wonderful athlete, most of her teammates were not. The pitchers walked most of the kids they faced. Hitters who swung the bat tended to strike out or bounce weak grounders to the infield. Most runs were actually scored through bases-loaded walks. So the odds favored taking every pitch.

Then, when that same dad's daughter was playing second base, an easy infield hit dribbled toward her. She picked it up and threw it to first. There would have been plenty of time to make the out, if the ball hadn't sailed ten feet over the first baseman's head. The runner advanced to second. The girl's father had a fit. "Never try to throw the runner out" he yelled. "Just toss it back to the pitcher." Again, he did have a point. With this team, a high percentage of throws made under pressure were not caught. The odds favored not doing it. Still, what was he teaching his daughter? Don't play the game. Don't take any chances, even if that's how you learn the skills that will eventually help you succeed. Just concentrate on minimizing your failures. It might have been good strategy for that one day, but it seems like a defeatist attitude for the long term.

It's natural for people to want to protect their children from struggle, failure and embarrassment. It's the right thing to do. Yet, quite often it's struggle, failure and embarrassment that teach us life's greatest lessons. That's why I probably learned more during my junior high years than at any time since. But that's another story.

Looking back on this incident makes me think about the advice people like to give seniors. After all, people's attitude toward children is usually reflected in their attitude toward seniors. When your parents get to a certain age, you tend to worry about them in the same way you did over your small kids. Ever since Shakespeare wrote that little speech about the seven ages of man, people have thought of old age as just a reprise of childhood.

I know they really mean well. But at the same time, I feel a little like I'm a kid being gently advised not to swing at a pitch.

My advice to kids – and their grandparents – is this: go ahead and swing at the pitch once in a while. You might miss, but at least you know that you're in the game. And that's more important.

Mobility: You've Got to Walk the Walk.

According to the Native American saying, you shouldn't judge a man until you've walked a mile in his moccasins. A few years ago, the truth of this was brought home to me. I came to understand my father a lot better after I started walking like he did.

It's not that my father wore moccasins. Before he retired, he wore mostly brown oxfords to work and sneakers in the garden. In his later years, he tended to favor awful-looking loafers with Velcro closures. But I think it's not the shoes that are important here, it's the walking.

Sometimes it seems like the story of a man's life can be read in his walk. There was a time when my father's walk was fluid and determined. He had the walk of a former Boy Scout hiker, of an outdoorsman, of a man who had done without a car during much of World War II. When I was in junior high, it meant a lot when he told me I was one of the few people who could walk fast enough to keep up with him.

In his later years, however, all that changed. He had bad knees, which for some reason he never got fixed like my mother did. His walk became more of a codger shuffle, and stairs were obviously painful.

I no longer aspired to walk like he did. In fact, I studiously avoided it. Then one day something happened. Maybe it was the yard work I did, or the bags of softener salt I carried down to the basement. Anyway, I spent an awful night with pain in my lower back and right hip. Next day, we left on a month-long vacation with our son Peter and his family. It began with a couple of agonizing plane rides, followed by many days of riding in a car over punishing Irish roads. Luckily, Irish pharmacies sell some very potent pain relievers over-the-counter. It wasn't easy, but I eventually managed to walk a lot of miles and see lots of beautiful Irish scenery. Sometimes I almost kept up with the rest of my family. And gradually, things settled down to normal, back-and-hip-wise.

Trying out my father's way of walking for a month gave me new insight into his life. And understanding your father better than before has got to be a good thing. But it's not like I plan to continue walking that way myself. The shuffle made famous on TV by Tim Conway is not the model I aspire to follow.

Instead, I've got a new mentor in mind. After watching our granddaughter, Meghan, and her teammates flit up and down the soccer field, I have decided that's the style of locomotion I plan to adopt. Hopefully, in the future I'll be able to say that you shouldn't judge me until you've run a few yards in my soccer cleats.

Simple Exercises Can Make You Live Longer

An item I saw in the paper recently proved something I've believed all along. Vices aren't really so bad for you as long as you choose them wisely – overeating, for example. According to a study by an aerobics research organization in Dallas, obese people who exercise have just half the death rate each year as thin people who don't exercise.

This has got to be wonderful news for those of us who have avoided the curse of being thin. Even if we don't currently get any exercise, at least being obese sounds like it counts as halfway to scoring a healthy lifestyle. All we need to do is find some suitable ways to do the other half – working out. Preferably, ways that are suitable for people who don't like to do anything very strenuous.

I quickly formed a committee to come up with a fitness program. None of the members are in the medical profession, but they all qualify as being obese. Here are some of the exercises they recommend:

1. Jumping to Conclusions.
Begin with your feet firmly on the ground. See how far your imagination can take you after hearing a short series of statements. You can try a variation of this exercise by letting your enthusiasm jump on (or off) the bandwagon.

2. Leap of Faith.
This is similar to the first exercise, except you don't need to hear anybody recite a series of statements. You can come up with them yourself. Caution: if your leap of faith involves politics or romance, you may land in hot water.

3. Sofa Curl.
Select a book as heavy as you can manage. Curl up on the sofa and read it through without stopping.

4. Pop-Can Pull.

Forcibly remove the tabs from a dozen cans during the course of an evening. This exercises the finger muscles and triceps. Follow this by repeatedly lifting the cans to your mouth, which is excellent for the biceps. Swallowing the contents of the cans uses many muscles in the throat while restoring essential fluids to the body. This works with beer cans too.

5. Acid Reflux Flex.

Jump out of bed in the middle of the night and try to breathe deeply through your seared windpipe. Repeat several times before morning.

6. Positive Spin.

Smooth out the inconsistencies in something said by a person you like.

7. Ironic Twist.

Firmly grasp the inconsistencies in something said by a person you don't like. Hold them up for all to see.

8. Eyebrow Lift.

Comment silently on those inconsistencies.

9. Thumb Press.

Sit with feet elevated. Hold a small plastic weight in your right hand, with your arm extended toward the TV. Use your thumb to press a series of buttons on the device. At the next commercial, repeat with your left hand.

One or two repetitions of these exercises each day should take care of the average obese person's needs or wants. We'll be able to prolong our lives while still enjoying them. That should show those skinny people that we know how to have our cake and eat it too. Hey, come to think of it, let's make that exercise number 10.

Enjoying Your Retirement Takes Disorderly Conduct

One night, with just an hour's notice, a couple we hadn't seen for ten years dropped in to visit. Of course, the news of their imminent arrival set off a spasm of dusting, vacuuming, and putting-away that made our house wonder what hit it. I don't think we needed to bother, because Jack and Irene seem to have developed an inspiring appreciation for disorder.

It wasn't always that way. Their lives used to be at least as orderly as anybody else's. Jack, an engineer, had started his own little manufacturing business. Irene, whom my wife has known since high school, took care of the books. If not humdrum, their lives were at least predictable. It was after they retired a few years ago that they began to appreciate the beauty of disorder in their lives. Although they moved to Florida, they didn't settle into a routine of spending their days playing golf and bridge with other retirees. The day after they moved into their new home, ten of their children and grandchildren arrived for a visit. That must have started things out on a fine note of creative chaos. Jack and Irene have continued in that vein ever since.

For half of every year, they travel the country in a motor home, dropping in on folks like us. There is no schedule or itinerary, except when they want to catch a cruise ship to Alaska or watch a hot air balloon festival in New Mexico.

They also seem to spend a lot of time traveling under their own power, via bike or canoe. Recently they taught some of their grandchildren how to windsurf.

When home in Florida, they delight in repeated trips to Epcot and Disney World. They described in wide-eyed detail the beauty of space shuttle launches they had seen. I can't think of anybody else who actually frequents all the tourist spots in their own neighborhood.

"I'll tell you a secret about retirement," Jack told us. *"It's busy — busier than working ever was."*

If they can ever find the time, I think these people should give a workshop on how to enjoy retirement. Part of their success must be the physical activity that helps preserve their health and vitality. Part of it is the time and effort they spend to be close to their extended family instead of cooped up with codgers in a retirement community. A big part of their enjoyment must come from the enthusiastic curiosity that makes them want to continually explore new parts of the world, and at the same time enables them to enjoy the surroundings in their own neighborhood as though seeing them for the first time.

The theme that underlies all of these things, I think, is learning to appreciate a certain amount of chaos. New experiences, spontaneous travel, challenging exercise — they all require us to step outside our daily routine. It seems that in retirement, things are reversed from before. To succeed, we need to learn how to impose disorder on our lives.

Good Advice from Two 75-Year-Olds

When political pundit William Safire bade farewell to his New York Times readers in 2005 after more than 3,000 columns, he made it clear that he was not retiring. Why not? After all, he was 75 years old at the time. Well, he explained that in part it was because of some advice he once got from James Watson, the Nobel Prize winner who helped discover the structure of DNA. Watson had said, "Never retire. Your brain needs exercise or it will atrophy."

So instead of retiring, Mr. Safire devoted his time to serving as chairman of the Dana Foundation – a group that encourages scientific research relating to the study of the brain and the ethical questions involved. It was a long stretch from being a right-wing opinion monger, language critic, and novelist to becoming a leader in the scientific community. But Mr. Safire figured that this kind of stretching is exactly what a person needs to do from time to time. He explained this point with another bit of advice: *"When you're through changing, you're through."*

It's interesting how two seemingly contradictory ideas really do agree. Don't retire. But don't be afraid to hang up your spurs either. The key is to move on to something new and challenging.

The two bits of advice he mentioned in his farewell column remind me of how a couple of similar insights had a powerful effect on my own career.

The first was something Somerset Maugham, the novelist, was supposed to have said on his 75th birthday. (75 seems to be the time for showing insight on aging). An interviewer asked him if 75 was a big milestone – maybe even a little frightening. *"Not at all,"* the author replied. *"The biggest birthday for a man is his 30th, because after that you can't pretend you're a boy anymore."*

Well, I had the misfortune to read that quote when I was 29 years old. It jolted me into looking at my life. Although by then I was the father of four, in many ways I was still boyishly waiting for life to begin.

Back when I was in college, the student placement office had fixed me up with a part-time job to help pay my tuition. After I graduated, the firm I was working for offered me a full time job. It wasn't in the field I had majored in, but I took it anyway. It was clean, easy, secure work. My bosses and co-workers were pleasant. Everything was fine, except that the work itself wasn't exactly satisfying to me. Well, I figured that was okay. Someday I would get into a field I could be passionate about.

All of a sudden, here I was at 29 and Somerset Maugham was breaking the news that I wouldn't be a boy much longer. I decided that by age 30 I should be in a career that actually mattered to me. It was hard to give up a secure position and start out fresh, but I took the plunge. After some effort, I was able to find work related to the major I had chosen in college. There was a slight cut in pay at first, but the other benefits were phenomenal.

Suddenly, I actually looked forward to going to work each day. No longer did a little case of sniffles keep me home. My attitude changed. My life changed. I stayed with that company for 26 years. I might have stayed longer, except for another pithy bit of insight. This one I came up with on my own.

After spending quite a while at the same low-level management job, I asked myself: *"If you haven't changed your position in ten years, shouldn't you consider the possibility that you might be dead?"*

I decided I preferred to feel alive. I took an early retirement from that corporation at age 55. However, like William Safire, I certainly didn't think of it as a real retirement. I started a little home-based business. Sure, it was a struggle. But again, the benefits were worth it. Meeting new challenges every day stimulates you mentally. Learning to repeatedly land on your feet has got to be good exercise for you physically.

I'm not saying that your post-retirement activity has to involve working in a regular kind of job. There are so many other opportunities to keep busy – Habitat for Humanity houses to build, Meals On Wheels to deliver, grandchildren to baby-sit, classes to take, memoirs to write.

The point is that, from first-hand experience, I can vouch for the value of Mr. Safire's attitude toward work. Retire early and often if you wish, but never really retire. Life is all about change, and when you're through changing, you're through. On the other hand, as long as you keep moving, growing, and learning – doing all those things that come so naturally to kids – you'll be young in the ways that really matter.

Fight to Expand the Menus

When young children go into a restaurant, they're often treated like little senior citizens. It seems like an awful way to treat innocent kids. I'm not just talking about the way some servers adopt a loud, overly enthusiastic, patronizing tone when talking to both kids and seniors. I'm referring to the way many eating places try to limit the menu choices for both groups.

Someone has decided that kids and seniors don't like the same things that normal people do. Kids are supposed to like chicken fingers, hot dogs, and macaroni and cheese. Those are about the only choices listed on their special menus, next to the riddles, games, and pictures to color. Seniors sometimes get their own sections on the menu too: smaller portions, limited selection. Apparently, like our grandchildren, we don't want anything particularly interesting. Also, kids are either assumed to be very impatient or items on their menu are very quick to prepare. As a result, servers bring out those meals twenty minutes before they feed the adults in the party. Like our grandchildren, seniors also are expected to eat early. By that I mean our senior specials are sometimes available only if we dine at about four or five o'clock, before the normal customers arrive.

We may have done plenty to deserve the treatment we get, but those poor kids haven't. We owe it to them to try to counter this trend. Otherwise, it might spread to other institutions besides eating places. For example, what if schools start limiting selections for the young in the way that some of them already do for elders?

For example, the college I graduated from eons ago came up with a program a while back that let people my age audit classes at no cost (provided they weren't filled up by paying students). This was a wonderful idea. But you should see the list of codger courses they suggested for us. Medieval history. Intermediate Latin. Victorian novelists. Preparing your will (which I'm sure emphasized the importance of leaving money to your alma mater). They were more than happy to mail out this short list to anyone interested in the program. But getting an actual catalog that included all the courses they offered to normal students was just about impossible. After all, why would a senior citizen be interested in learning about things like film-making, chemistry, or computer programming?

If educational institutions continue this trend of following the example of restaurants by reducing choices for both youngsters and oldsters, there soon may no longer be a whole lot of subjects available for children to study. One or two sports will suffice for gym class. Classrooms will feature just history and multiplication. Then the kids may go home to find that Sesame Street is brought to them every day by the same letter.

To keep this from happening to our grandchildren, we seniors should do everything we can to fight efforts to limit choices because of age. If we succeed in reversing the trend for our own age group, maybe it will help the kids too. So when the car salesman steers you to the four-door sedan, insist on looking at the sporty convertible. When the travel agent touts Branson or St. Petersburg, ask about whitewater rafting. When the dentist suggests a crown, find out if he also does tongue piercing.

Mind you, I'm not saying you must actually buy the convertible, shoot the rapids, or allow any part of yourself to be pierced. The important thing is to expand the menus. Get people out of the habit of assuming they know what we want. We all live in rooms with walls that keep slowly moving in on us if we don't constantly work at pushing them back. Let's push back. We've gotta do it for the kids.

A Valuable Lesson to Learn from a Computer

I think I'm learning some valuable lessons from my computer – and I don't even have any software to teach me Spanish or calculus or how to play blackjack. The computer is teaching me by example.

After working hard for a couple of years, the machine started to get a little neurotic. It would lose its train of thought in the middle of a routine task, or confess that it had just performed an illegal action and must be shut down as punishment. Pretty soon, it was on the verge of psychosis, flashing blue screens screaming about fatal errors. It needed drastic psychotherapy.

Mike, my computer guru, explained that over time a computer builds up a lot of extra connections and procedures and leftover pieces of business from all the jobs it has thought about. Eventually it starts to feel confused and overwhelmed. It needs to start over. Mike completely erased the hard drive and set up the operating system afresh. After that, I had to reinstall the software I use. Strangely, the computer now has only about a quarter of the programs that it did before. I was amazed at the number of things I used to think I needed, but decided I didn't when faced with the bother of setting them up again. Needless to say, the computer seems to be much happier and better adjusted than before.

If I let my attention zoom out from my computer to the room in which it sits, I can see the need for a similar treatment. The clutter in my office would dismay a Feng Shui consultant and most likely infuriate the Fire Marshall. When I attempt to clean it out, I'm tripped up (both figuratively and literally) by all this stuff I used to think I needed. Maybe the answer is to treat the room as I did the hard drive – clear the place out completely, haul everything to a dumpster, and then bring back only what I decide is really needed.

Zooming out still further, what if I apply the same principle to my life in general? Do I really need to belong to all those organizations, go to all those meetings, and maintain all those "laborsaving" pieces of equipment? If I were to put everything in my life out on the lawn in a giant garage sale, how much of it would I bother to buy back myself?

It's not just a matter of physical stuff cluttering things up. Like the computer, we tend to accumulate connections and attitudes and memories that interfere with our contentment. Short of erasing our mental hard drives through electroshock therapy, I wonder if there's a way to start fresh.

Do I really need to make X-number of dollars a year? Do I really need to win this argument? Do I really need to persuade this person to do what I want? I'll bet I can get along without a lot of the things that currently seem important. Who knew that the greatest lesson we could learn from a computer might be how to forget?

Old-Time Weather Wisdom Updated for Today

Remember the days before we got our weather forecasts from TV? We had no well-coiffed experts equipped with an endless supply of Doppler diagrams and satellite pictures capable of pinpointing every incoming cloud. Instead, we tried to predict the weather from bits of folk wisdom based on clues that nature provided. Often, these sayings came in verse form to make them easier to remember.

My grandparents were good at that sort of thing. I guess they needed to know everything that helped them understand nature in order to wrest a living from their small farm. In turn, my parents tried to pass these bits of wisdom on to me, but without a lot of success.

I remember there was some kind of saying about woolly bear caterpillars. The width of the colored band around their middle was supposed to tell you how cold the coming winter would be. Those of us who were brought up in the city didn't really run into that many woolly bear caterpillars. I was vaguely aware of the saying about "Red sky at night" but I was never sure whether it was followed by "sailors' delight" or "sailors take fright." (I had an uncle who had been a sailor, but he was never around much in the evening for me to observe.) Then there was "Rain before seven, sun by eleven." Or was it the other way around? The trouble is that today's urban lifestyle makes it hard to relate to a lot of those old weather sayings. I think that's too bad. Part of our culture is being lost. What we should do is replace the old sayings with new ones that modern people can relate to. Here are a few bits of new folk wisdom that may prove helpful in the years ahead:

Night sky black with dots of white–
Things are pretty much all right.
Night sky glowing reddish brown–
The power plant is melting down.

* * * *

Never mind what pilots say,
watch what flight attendants do instead.
Coffee cups filled all the way,
mean bumpy weather's just ahead.

* * * *

Summer party out of doors,
down the pelting cloudburst pours.
Summer party held inside,
air conditioner circuit's fried.

* * * *

Imply your spouse is growing old,
and things will soon get very cold,
but several carats worth of "ice"
can turn the climate rather nice.

* * * *

When penguins all are bleached snow-white
and blisters cover each seal's pup,
then stay indoors except at night,
until the Ozone Hole heals up.

* * * *

Picking home-grown tropic fruits,
water-skiing down your street,
bikinis worn as business suits--
global warming can be neat!

* * * *

If hot air's swirling all around
and clouds of fog blot out the sun
and you can't escape a droning sound
Election season has begun.

* * * *

Aren't those easier to understand than woolly bears? Once we get the hang of using these updated pieces of old-time folk wisdom, I bet we'll find them just as helpful as our grandparents found the original ones.

Ringing in the New Year with the Owls and Larks

For several years, we celebrated New Year's in a pretty strange way. At first blush, it seems crazy. Yet, in my continuing effort to try to find logic and purpose behind what we do, I've come to the conclusion that maybe it did make profound sense. What we were doing was celebrating the New Year with both the owls and the larks. People who tend to stay up late are often described as owls, whereas those who get up really early are called larks. It's some kind of genetic thing. Well, we've got friends in both camps, so we rang in the New Year twice.

First we drove an hour south of our home to observe New Year's Eve with three other couples. My brother-in-law was the ringleader of this group. We would leave this party about one o'clock, and be in bed by two. Then we were up before six and drove an hour to the east in order to toast the sunrise with another group of our friends, most of whom we had met through the Chamber of Commerce. The two celebrations were as different as – well, night and day. Each was good in its own way.

The owls lived up to their name not only by staying up late, but by being relatively serious, conservative, and wise. Their conversation was very pleasant but sedate. Hors d'oeuvres were ample, delicious, and traditional. So was the ham dinner, followed by the annual game of Pictionary. At midnight, there would be a toast, but before that there wasn't a lot of drinking.

Next morning, we joined the larks. They lived up to THEIR name not only by getting up early, but by manifesting exuberance and happiness. The first order of business was to toast the sunrise with Champagne. For some reason, they felt they must do this while standing on ice – sometimes on a river, sometimes a lake. Then we repaired to a nice restaurant for breakfast and a Bloody Mary or two. Conversation was wild, unpredictable, and creative. Sometimes they returned to the lake after breakfast for some ice fishing. By that time, however, my wife and I were ready for home and a nap.

Why did we start out the year by subjecting ourselves to such an exhausting schedule? Some might think it was due to an insatiable desire for constant partying. This is not true – at least in my case. (My wife, I'm not so sure.) The owl group helped keep us grounded, while the lark group helped keep us open. At first glance, it might seem like an age thing. It's true that our lark friends were younger than the owls by ten or fifteen years on the average. But my wife and I were even three or four years older than the owls, so where did that put us? We should have been the buzzards or something.

I think if you want to stay young while enjoying the benefits of maturity, you need to keep in touch with both your inner owl and lark. How else can a person hope to be wise as an owl and happy as a lark? Few people seem to manage both at the same time, but we can always hope. A few more New Years might just do it.

It's Time to Resist the Last Bastion of Discrimination

Let's say some guy loses control of his car and crashes it through the window of a store on Main Street. If the driver happens to be African-American or Chinese or Hispanic, news reports won't mention the fact. That might imply that his race was somehow the reason for his bad driving. Thank heaven our society has gotten past that sort of stereotyping.

But if the driver is up in years, you can be very sure the news reports will say that an elderly man lost control of his car and crashed into the building. Oh, of course he did. He was elderly.

A dozen people may succumb to West Nile Virus or Lyme's Disease or Bird Flu. Again, if one of them was elderly the reporters will feel obliged to mention that detail. Like, the virus isn't necessarily that serious because there were extenuating circumstances – the person was elderly. The other victims may all have been blonde, or all college graduates, or all left-handed, but there seems to be no impulse to link their fate to those things.

If you have a decent driving record, car rental companies will do business with you regardless of your race, religion, or political affiliation. But if you're over 70, some companies will charge you more than a younger person. If you're over 80, some companies won't rent to you at all.

In the corporate world, companies that wouldn't dream of discriminating based on race or gender still routinely avoid hiring or promoting seniors. Age-discrimination is very hard to prove and almost never punished. It seems obvious that some kind of Senior Rights Movement is long overdue. So how should we launch it?

Well, marches worked pretty well for the Civil Rights folks. But I'm thinking that a 54-mile trek like the 1965 march from Selma to Montgomery is a little too ambitious. Going from Sun City to Phoenix is shorter, and might be more appropriate. Somebody should organize a march there. Perhaps, in this case, the marchers could be permitted to use golf carts. For those seniors who don't happen to spend the winter in that area, maybe we could just wave some banners and shout some slogans while we get our mall-walking exercise in our own home towns. If the mall security people hassle us, that'll make for some good photo opportunities.

Undocumented workers once tried to demonstrate their numbers and influence legislation by staging a "Day Without Immigrants." Thousands stayed home from work across the country. Unfortunately, not many seniors have jobs to stay home from. But we could hold a "Day Without Seniors" with respect to shopping. It might be a real eye-opener, at least for pharmacies or stores that sell support hose and comfortable shoes.

Finally, feminists used to draw a lot of attention to their cause by publicly burning their bras. I wonder, are Depends flammable? Come on, people! Seniors are the only group still suffering widespread discrimination. Rise up from your recliners and join the fight for Codger Power!

What We Should Learn from Stem Cells

When I was little, most of what I learned came from those who were bigger than me. My parents taught me the rules of life, my teachers taught me the multiplication tables, and the school bully taught me to walk home in a convoy with some friends.

Now that I've attained seniorhood, most of what I learn seems to come from people or things that are smaller than me. From my grandchildren when they were infants, I relearned how to giggle without inhibition.

Then there was the ladybug that perched on the outside of my windshield and held on for miles no matter how fast I drove. From her, I learned strength, determination, and when to let go. (She somehow was smart enough to let go at exactly the right time – just before the weather made me turn on those deadly windshield wipers.) And now, according to some articles I've seen, the greatest lesson of all may come from the smallest teacher of all, a single cell. A stem cell, to be specific.

It turns out that stem cells hold the promise of curing a lot of diseases and injuries because of their unique ability to turn themselves into any kind of tissue or organ in our bodies. But these medical aspects aren't the reason why I'm bringing up stem cells. I don't think I currently need an injection of them to fix any major organ in my body. (Knock on wood!) I just think they have a lot to teach us by example.

Think about it. Stem cells are what biologists call undifferentiated. They're like a blank canvas. They can turn into anything. As a result, their DNA is essentially immortal. Later, after they decide whether to become muscle, bone, liver, or skin, they start to get set in their ways. They change their appearance, their behavior, their whole outlook. And then they start to age.

Once cells get set in their ways, the shoelace-like telemeres at the end of their DNA get a little shorter each time they divide. The cells can only divide so many times and then they get old and can't carry on any more.

Isn't that sort of what happens to us? We start out a blank canvas. We can develop an enthusiasm for almost anything. But in school we start to specialize – in math or language or sports or whatever. Then we get a job and specialize further. We join unions, chambers of commerce, and political parties. Even our hobbies become specialized. We turn into bowlers or watercolor painters or TV addicts. The more we specialize and harden, and the less we are open to experimenting with other lifestyles, the more we age. It seems to me that the antidote to aging is to adopt the philosophy of a stem cell. We should become undifferentiated, open to everything. This can help no matter what stage of life we happen to be in right now.

Kids nowadays would benefit from more undifferentiated playtime. Instead of all those organized sports with coaches and referees, they could play pickup softball or kick the can, making up the rules themselves like my friends and I used to do.

Young adults need to be flexible and undifferentiated too. Even the best job can suddenly disappear, and entire career fields become obsolete. People who are open to change are better suited to jump to a new one.

We seniors, especially, need to avoid getting too set in our ways. We need that fountain of youth effect more than anybody. We could start by giving up our recliner once in a while in favor of a bike seat or deck chair or roller coaster. We could take a new look at our wardrobe, diet, and politics. We could seek out new friends, and then introduce them to our old ones. Always being open to new possibilities makes us undifferentiated, just like that little stem cell. It's the key to staying ever young.

Not Very Much Pay, but Great Benefits!

At an age well after most people retired, I started a new full-time job. Actually, my wife and I have been job-sharing it. Just as in the movie of the same name, our job involves Driving Miss Daisy.

The job also includes walking Miss Daisy, feeding Miss Daisy, and doing anything else that Miss Daisy requires. So far, what she mostly wants is for us to cuddle her, rub her tummy, and play tug-of-war with her.

Miss Daisy is a little bundle of fluffy white fur. She's a Cavapoo, which is not as bad as it sounds. It means her father was a Poodle and her mother a Cavalier King Charles Spaniel. (I wonder why humans don't adopt similar names to show their ethnic heritage. My wife would be an Irishgerm and I'd be an Engdutchgerm. Oh, I guess that's why.)

Like most people who start working at our age, we took the job not so much for the pay as for the benefits. In fact, the pay so far has been in the high negative numbers, involving doggie food, toys, grooming, and vet care.

When Miss Daisy was a puppy, many of the benefits of living with her involved her love of play as well as chasing and returning things. And she has always expressed an eager friendship for our kids, grandkids, guests, and neighbors. Now that she's 11 years old, the benefits tend to focus on the healthful exercise that comes with walking her several times a day, and the warmth she brings on a wintry night by lying across the back of your neck while you sit on the couch watching TV.

Finally, working for Miss Daisy requires us to give more thought to planning our lives. Instead of just jumping into our car and going off on the spur of the moment, we actually have to do a little planning. A short shopping trip means we have to remember to set her up in the office, with a supply of food and water. Long trips require arranging a place for her to stay (which isn't much of a problem, given the positive reaction of our family and friends to her). But the mental exercise involved in the additional planning and logistics required may help us stave off senility for a little bit longer.

So let's add up the benefit package that comes with working for Miss Daisy: More new friends. More discipline in our lives. More physical exercise to lengthen our lives. More mental exercise to postpone our appointment with Mr. Alzheimer. I'd say this has got to be one of the best jobs I ever landed.

All Seniors Should Show This Kind of Faith in the Younger Generation

I was sitting on a park bench last January 1st, watching the world go by, when an old man came shuffling down the path. He had a long white beard, wore a white robe, and carried a walking stick. Wearily, he sat down on the bench across from me. Just then a child came skipping up and joined us.

"Are you the New Year?" asked the old timer.

"Yes, sir. I hope you don't mind my taking

over from here," the youngster said shyly.

"I'm VERY glad to meet you, young fella!" said the gentleman, extending his gnarled hand.

"So, how have things been going?" the kid asked.

"Not so hot, I'm afraid. People are still killing each other for the dumbest of reasons – religion or tribe or because someone's got a couple of bucks in their pocket. And they're not taking good care of the planet they live on. Greed is everywhere. Why, just last week I even saw a beautiful religious holiday get turned into an orgy of commercialism. And just a few hours ago, a lot of people got soused for no other reason than that they were awaiting your arrival. I guess I haven't done a very good job."

"Gee, I'm sorry. But don't worry. I'll fix things. I've got a lot of plans!"

I couldn't help but join their conversation. *"How are you going to change the world?"* I asked the youngster.

"Well, I sure want to do something about that killing stuff. People will have to stop fighting and start respecting each other. I'll tell everybody they have to play nice."

"That's very good advice," I replied. *"How are you going to make it happen?"*

"Well, on my very first day I'll ask people to make some resolutions to behave better than they did in the old year. No disrespect intended to you, sir, of course."

"Of course," said the bearded man.

"Next, I'm going to teach people all through the year with some special lessons. For example, in January I'll have a special day that teaches people about brotherhood and respecting each other regardless of things like race. Then in February, I'll have a day devoted to love."

I opened my mouth to point out that we already had Martin Luther King Day and Valentine's Day, but the old man interrupted before I could speak. "Those sound like great ideas, son," he said with a wink at me. "What else have you come up with?"

"Well, I figure that people can always draw inspiration from their respected leaders, so I'm going to have a President's Day next. And some time in Spring, which is the season of rebirth, it seems like a good time to celebrate Christ's resurrection from the dead and the Jews' escape to freedom. But I don't want people to be too serious all the time, so around the first of April I plan to lighten things up with a day devoted to silly jokes."

I decided not to tell him about Income Tax Day later that month. No sense spoiling his euphoria. "Then what's next?" I asked.

"Well, I think we should have days honoring mothers and fathers, and also one to remember friends and relatives who have passed on. And a day celebrating the establishment of the country's government would help remind people of the principles they should live by. A day honoring the dignity of working people and another one thanking those who served their country would be kind of inspiring too.

"Then, as we get near the end of my year, we'll have a

very special day thanking God for all our blessings. Finally, just after the wintry days begin to lengthen again making the future look brighter, we'll celebrate the birth of Christ. And on the last night of my tour of duty, I'll throw a little party to celebrate all the improvements."

"Son, those sound like great learning experiences for the people on this planet," said the old man. "Go to it, and good luck!"

The youngster went skipping off down the path. I turned to the old guy and said, "He's so naive! He doesn't have a chance and you know it. Why didn't you tell him?"

The bearded guy slowly shook his head. "My friend, the biggest sin we old folks can commit is to rob the younger generation of hope. And besides, his ideas sound pretty good the way he explains them. Just maybe people will learn from this coming year's holidays and will start behaving better. Who knows? He may be the first one of us who is actually able to pull it off."

I got up and ambled off down the path after the youngster. It'll be interesting to see how he does.

In a Bed, Size Really Does Matter
(The Bed Size, Not That Other Thing)

One lesson the younger generations need to be learning as a result of these stressful times is that bigger isn't necessarily better. In fact, bigger is often worse. And that doesn't just apply to voracious corporations, suburban McMansions with mortgages to match, gas-guzzling cars, and diabetes-prone obese bodies. It applies to simple things like furniture too.

My wife, Mickey, and I are still using the bed we bought when we got married in 1955. There have been a number of new mattresses over the years, but the beautiful maple headboard and footboard, like the marriage itself, is still pretty sturdy. Ironically, although our style of bed is referred to as "full sized," or a "double bed," it's sort of a midget compared to the queen and king-sized beds everybody buys today. I really can't imagine why people think it's better to sleep like kings and queens. Are royal families noted for being particularly happy or well rested?

Our smaller bed has plenty of room. On one side, there's space for Mickey's book, reading glasses, and portable book light. In addition, there's usually a small white dog, Miss Daisy, near the bottom. On the other half of the bed there's room for – well, Mickey and me. Cuddling is not just affectionate, it's more or less necessary.

Recently we spent some time visiting a bed and breakfast in northern Minnesota. It was in a beautiful log building. There were wonderful breakfasts accompanied by fascinating conversations with our host and hostess. Walks in the woods. A lake view out the window of our room. And a big king-sized bed. All but the last part was great.

It can be scary to wake up at night and think your partner has left you, when it turns out she's just a few yards away in the same bed. To cuddle, you must squirm across an immense distance and hope to meet somewhere before morning. As nice as the B&B was, once we got home there was a certain feeling of "Ahhh, now that's better" when getting into our own bed.

I can't help but wonder if today's higher divorce rate is related to the loss of intimacy caused by oversized beds. Or maybe the financial stress of having to buy bigger houses to accommodate them.

The misguided popularity of these giant beds may be partly due to their names. Queen-size. King-size. Sounds really spiffy. Why don't we change to more accurate names? After all, they're not really used that often by actual royalty. Let's call queen-size "triple beds" and king-size "quadruple beds." That more accurately describes their size relative to double beds.

Adopting this name change should help clarify furniture shopping. If your available living space or chosen lifestyle calls for three or four people sharing a bed, then by all means get one of the big ones. But if you're a couple, I advise you to buy the old fashioned double bed. Cuddling is good for you.

The Depression's Lessons

Having been born in the 1930s should give me a big advantage in dealing with any current hard times I run into today. Let's see, what things did I learn during the Great Depression? They might possibly include some lessons that could help the whole country.

Learn from others – just don't copy them

My mother used to tell the story of one of the first things I learned as a result of the Depression – although she didn't approve of it. I was just three years old. Some laborers from the WPA (Works Progress Administration) were repairing our street, and I followed along, watching them with fascination. When I returned to the house, I excitedly shared with my mother a new word I had just learned: *"Mama – D*MN!"*

It had seemed like such a great word to me because it was used so enthusiastically and so often by those big guys. But it definitely didn't please my mother and she banned it from my vocabulary. Now, however, I'm inclined to use it every time I read about depressing things in the news like foreclosures, layoffs, bankruptcies, and rip-offs. It doesn't seem to help much, but it does let me blow off steam. Maybe it also helps me feel united with those hard-working guys from the 30s who taught it to me.

What might help the entire country, though, would be to set up some modern equivalent of the crew that I watched that day. Not only did the WPA create desperately needed jobs, but an awful lot of nice roads, sidewalks, and parks soon displayed that WPA logo pressed into the concrete. Our country could use more of that kind of effort today.

Make a Little Do a Lot

The next lesson I learned from the Depression was that you could do a lot with a little. It was something I saw every day, particularly in the summer. My dad delivered fuel oil for a living, so we had to coast through the summer on what he made during the winter. There was very little money for food, clothing, or entertainment.

I saw lots of examples of how to accomplish the necessities of life with very little in the way of resources. One I especially remember is how we got our first refrigerator.

I was in kindergarten. In those days, our scanty food supply was kept in an old icebox. That's right, kids, it was cooled with actual blocks of ice delivered by the iceman every few days. There was no way we could afford a refrigerator. Even if credit cards had existed, my folks wouldn't have gone into debt like that. But my mother thought hard and managed to get us one without spending any money.

Back then, companies sponsored dozens of contests that you entered by writing a 25-word-or-less essay about why the sponsor's product was wonderful.

Think of it. Twenty-five words is only the length of that last paragraph. To make your entry stand out above thousands of others, you had to be really good at doing a lot with a little. My mother was a master at that. Just twenty-five words and a three cent stamp, and we won a glossy white refrigerator!

All of us need to relearn that ability to accomplish a lot with very little. We need to figure out innovative ways to get what we want without buying on credit. And wouldn't it be great if our political leaders could learn how to make do with just a limited number of words and dollars? If only all the people of today could have learned at my mother's knee!

Walk It Off

In the 1930s, people got lots of exercise. Yet, nobody paid money to go to a gym unless they were trying to become a professional boxer. We walked to the grocery store and church and school. If we traveled further, the journey started with a walk to the streetcar or bus line. And the average weight of Americans was much lower than today.

The lesson? Walk or bike where you're going whenever it's possible. And it's possible more often than you probably think. If we all start doing that, the price of gas will shrink. And so will our national obesity epidemic. There's nothing like being thin to help you get through almost any sort of tight spot.

Good luck in applying the lessons of the 30s. They're another example of the new ideas we can pick up from times – and people – that are old.

Conversion to Coprolite

In my mid-sixties, I underwent a conversion and became a Coprolite. Actually, it wasn't so much a conversion as a return to the fold. My parents and grandparents were all Coprolites too. You may be assuming that the Coprolites are a religious group, like the Mennonites or Carmelites. That's not the case. Coprolite is actually a sort of mineral that you can buy in many rock shops.

Coprolite is fossilized old poop. So when I became a Coprolite, it had to do with my realizing that I was something of a fossilized old poop myself. By the way, most of the Coprolite sold in rock shops comes from dinosaurs, so that was another indication of what I was turning into.

I certainly wasn't always that way. As a toddler, I was the cutest little kid, with curly blond hair and a winning smile. There are even pictures to prove it. Every day was filled with enthusiastic fun.

I started kindergarten one January in a school district that had both December and June graduating classes. After I was in kindergarten just half a year, my family moved to a regular once-a-year school system and I found myself up in first grade. From then on, I was always the youngest kid in my class. Also the skinniest.

I was married at just 20, a father at 21. My wife Mickey and I were generally among the youngest members of any social group or PTA to which we belonged.

Somewhere along the line, all of that changed. My blonde curls are long gone. My youthful freckles have been replaced by some kind of scaly dots that the doctor seems to enjoy spraying with liquid nitrogen. We tend to be the oldest couple among the people we hang out with. And I'm definitely not the skinniest among them. But I'm determined that one thing doesn't need to change with age. That's the part about filling every day with enthusiastic fun. If I'm to be a Coprolite at this stage of life, let me embrace being a fossilized old poop and make the most of it.

Despite our somewhat churchy-sounding name, the Coprolites won't be knocking on your door to hand out leaflets. You won't hear us proselytizing on a Sunday morning radio show. If you're ready to be one of us, just accept who and what you are and enjoy it!

What to Know About Opinions

Maturity comes when you realize that other people's opinions aren't all that important. Wisdom comes when you realize that yours aren't either.

I originally intended to expand on this thought, but come to think of it, those two sentences sum up everything you need to know about the subject.

"One" Should Mean United, Not Alone

I started life as an only child, I was usually the new kid in grade school (at six different schools, three in one year), and as a devoted non-athlete I was not the most popular guy in high school. But all lonely aspects of life went away big time when I married Mickey and we went on to have six children, eleven grandchildren, and eleven great-grandchildren. Boisterous family life definitely makes you feel one with something much bigger than yourself.

Now that I'm in my mid-80s, I've learned even a few more things about being one with someone or something else. It's a little hard to explain, but these days when I see anyone else, whether family member, friend, or complete stranger, I feel a new kind of bond and warmth. And when I think of God or the universe, I also feel a closer connection than I did before.

At first, this worried me, making me wonder if it was a sign that I was soon about to leave this life for the next. Nah, I'm pretty sure that's not the case. My parents both lived into their mid-90s, and I fully intend to break the century mark.

I think this new feeling of unity is simply a benefit that comes with age. When you're old enough, the things that separate you diminish and the things that unite you grow larger. "One" no longer means you're just one person, and alone. "One" means you're one with others, and one with the universe. If you're not old enough to have received this revelation, be patient. And when it comes to you, embrace and enjoy it to the hilt!

Try Something Brand New – or Really Old!

If you want to have the most fun in your retirement years, a great way is to try something brand new, something you never experienced before. An equally great way is to repeat something so old that you often used to enjoy it many years ago. Either approach works.

The "new" opens you up to exciting, stimulating, never-before-seen experiences. Visit a place you've never been before, try a food you've never tasted, attend a play you've never seen, listen to some unfamiliar music. The total novelty of the experience can greatly enhance the delight it brings you.

The "old" brings back some of the most enjoyable moments of your life. Hear music by the band that excited you as a teen, play "Duck Duck Gray Duck" again with your childhood friends, visit the lake or pool where you learned to swim, indulge in the kind of dessert your mother made that was your absolute favorite.

Just imagine how intriguing it could be if you experimented with combining something brand new with something really old in your life at the same time.

When you're dining out at your long-time favorite restaurant, try ordering something you've never, ever eaten there before. Or if you decide to go out to enjoy a meal that's been your favorite dish for years, get it at a restaurant you've never visited in the past. While strolling through an exotic new locale enjoying the scenery, have a favorite old Tarzan or Lone Ranger book from your childhood playing on some headphones. Program your new car's wizardly electronic dashboard to play a selection of old-fashioned music that you could have heard at your high school homecoming dance. Use a new computer to shop for antiques. Together with your spouse or some long-time friend, take a class in an exotic brand-new craft. Combining something new with something old has got to be a very special experience!

Learning to be open to both the new and old in life is what enables you to have the wisdom that comes with age plus the excitement that comes with youth. Don't settle for just one. Go for both!

How You Relate Might Depend on the Date

The way you relate to other people and to the world in general seems to depend in part on your age. Most people go through three distinct phases as they progress through life. A brief summary of them might be "fun, run, and one."

Fun

As a child, you're pretty much focused on having fun. What you love most are things like playing games, watching cartoons, or romping in the park. Much further down on your list are doing your homework, helping around the house, or learning new skills. Your relationship with friends largely focuses on enjoying the things you do spontaneously together.

Run

After you become an adult, you're quite a bit more serious, and you become pretty determined to run your own life. You want to work in the kind of job you pick out, marry the partner you love, and bring up children who follow all the rules you teach them. And at this age, competition becomes serious in your work life – competing with other companies for sales and with your co-workers for promotions.

One

In your later years, you may feel a powerful transformation in how you relate to people and nature. Competition is largely in the past and the people you see each day are mostly friends or family, not rivals – so you have a much stronger feeling of being one with them. But it goes beyond that. Even people you've just met can instill a feeling of togetherness in you. In addition to this attitude toward people, you may also develop a profound new sense of "oneness" with God and the universe. This feeling (which hit me in my 80's) can bring a remarkable sense of peace and belonging.

You've undoubtedly heard about the many losses that aging can bring – physical abilities that diminish, old friends and relatives who are lost, income that fades after retirement. But that one big gain that may come – feeling "one" with the people close to you and feeling "one" with the universe and its creator – can make a tremendous positive difference. Who would have thought that growing old could help bring about a fresh new perspective on life? It's important to continue to take advantage of what you have learned in all three phases of your life. Have FUN every day. Be sure to RUN your life as well as possible. And especially, open yourself up to being ONE with people, nature, and God.

Love Is God

The most important lesson anyone can learn about how to make life wonderful right up to the very end is an understanding of what love is all about. It's a long, ongoing process.

In the throes of my first crush, I was convinced that I was experiencing love as deeply as any human ever could. By the time I got married at the ripe old age of 20, I knew infinitely more about love. Now, in my mid-80s, I realize how little I still knew back then. I figure that I may really understand all about love in another decade or two. In the meantime, here's a progress report on what I've learned so far.

When I love, I shortchange both my beloved and myself unless I love her completely. How does a person love completely? By loving with body, mind, and spirit.

I start by loving with passion – all the ways my body knows how to love. The sight of her face and figure starts my blood racing. The sound of her voice makes my ears perk up with pleasure. Her scent makes my nostrils flare. The texture of her skin and the taste of her lips make me snuffle and snort and feel the urge to paw the ground with my hooves. To protect her, I would climb the Empire State Building and swat at planes like King Kong in that classic movie.

Next, I love her with intimacy – all the ways my mind knows how to love. I want to know how she feels about things. What makes her laugh, what makes her cry, what outrages her, what brings out her sense of play? I delight in every new facet that I discover. At the same time, I want to share with her everything there is to know about me. What fun it is to frolic like dolphins through each other's personalities!

Finally, I love her with what I call (for lack of a better word) commitment – the way that my soul knows how to love. I imagine that a spirit operates very simply. It's a little like an electric switch – the switch is open, or the switch is closed. Or maybe it's like a computer chip – the value is zero, or the value is one. I love this person, or I do not. If the switch is set to "love," there's a bridge between us. Because a spirit isn't tied to space and time, it's impossible to pin down just when I threw this switch – maybe when we first met, maybe after many years together, maybe before we were born. By the same token, if I do throw the switch to "love," I don't have a way to go back later and change it to "not love." There is no "later" for a spirit, since it is not tied to time. If I throw the switch, she has no need to keep earning my love. Anyone who "falls out of love" never did love with spirit.

Loving with passion doesn't require anything from us. That's why it's called "passion," as in "passive." It just happens. Loving with intimacy can only happen if we let it happen. We have to lower our natural barriers before we can let someone see into all the corners of our thoughts and emotions. Loving with commitment, I think, can happen only if we take positive action, and choose to flip that switch.

The famous "lovers" we read about in the tabloids these days seem to limit themselves pretty much to passion, the easiest, least-involved stage of love. The earnest characters in romantic novels and soap operas may blend passion and intimacy. But the great lovers of the world are those ordinary people who love in all three ways: passion, intimacy, and commitment – body, mind, and spirit.

I've been talking about love between sexual partners. But I don't mean to downplay the love that you have for your child, your sister, your friend, or your bowling team. Love for these other people is also vitally important to you. It works pretty much the same way, only without the snuffling, hoof-stomping, and airplane-swatting.

There's one more aspect of love that we need to consider. St. John's Gospel tells us that "God is love." What does that mean?

One theoretical version of the creation story goes something like this: The all-powerful entity that exploded the universe into existence is the Person we call God the Father. Because He is omniscient, He has an absolutely perfect understanding of everything that exists – including himself. His mental image of himself is such a perfect reflection that it stands on its own as another Self. This Second Person is sometimes called "The Word" (perhaps because a word is a mental symbol of something). Anyway, these two have such perfect understanding, acceptance and love for each other that this takes on form too, becoming the Third Person – the Holy Spirit. According to this theoretical explanation, it was inevitable that God would take the form of a Trinity.

So we can think of God as a combination of physical power, mental understanding, and spiritual acceptance and union. Darned if that doesn't sound pretty much like the three sides of human love! But isn't it really presumptuous to say that "God is Love," as though He's imitating one of our human characteristics? I believe it makes more sense to think of it the other way around. Love is God – translated down to human scale... a gift sent to help us understand.

Body, Mind, and Spirit

Passion is the way my body knows
how to love you. Its sweetest pains
hammer at my senses, and in its throes
I'd climb a skyscraper and swat at planes.

Being intimate is how my mind
shows its love. I deeply want to view
every thought you have and even find
the nerve to share my secret thoughts with you.

My spirit adds commitment to the mix.
Since spirits are not bound by time,
when mine decides to love it really sticks,
and makes our love eternally sublime.

These three are all I have to offer you.
If I find more, though, you will have those too.